LOVE YOU
love
YOUR LIFE

Please Note:
This book contains references to
suicide, loss, grief and mental health.

NAOMI VICTORIA

LOVE YOU love YOUR LIFE

LIFE LESSONS TO DISCOVER YOUR INNER HAPPY

I dedicate this book to you, the reader, for dreaming that
there can be more to life and taking steps to make it happen.
No matter how dark the day, hope and possibility
will see you through. If I can do it, so can you.

Mum, Dad, Nick, this is for you. Thank you for all
the beautiful memories and your incredible guidance
and for lighting the way, always.

The *seeds* of this book were *planted* many moons ago...

HOPE

HAPPY EVER AFTER

MY FAIRY TALE LIFE...

Once upon a time in a distant place I dreamed of...

Sunshine, happy days and flower-filled fields and prince charming that would rock up on his horse (or more like a Range Rover) and sweep me away.

I played with dolls and imagined a 'perfect' life like Barbie and Ken in her three-storey mansion with a pool on top, where I could rearrange furniture and change their styles every single day, without a worry in the world.

JUST HAPPY FAMILIES

A life of heartfelt bliss where I could have everything I asked for and more... where I would be held, loved and cherished. Where there were fluffy clouds and rainbows and I would be surrounded by Care Bears and happy songs...

Then I was forced to grow up!

"Over the Rainbow" by Israel "IZ" Kamakawiwo'ole

WHAT ABOUT YOUR HAPPY EVER AFTER?

When you are sitting in your own thoughts, do you ever dream of how life could be?

Do you ever wish you could be happier, wealthier, healthier, more successful, prettier, thinner, fitter, and smarter? I could go on.

Do you wish you could just sail off into the sunset without a care in the world?

Believing more is possible is a REALLY good thing to do! BUT...

Sabotaging who you are and not feeling good enough right in this very moment is NOT!

There's a big difference between working on yourself, living a life of your dreams, building confidence, courage, belief and beating yourself up for not feeling or being good enough.

If you are currently berating yourself in any way shape or form...

- Feeling deflated
- Playing small
- Or a shadow of yourself

I am here to help you discover your own inner happy to support you to create a life you really love. So let's get started.

POSSIBILITY

CONTENTS

PART 1

LIFE CURVEBALLS

"The Circle of Life" by Elton John

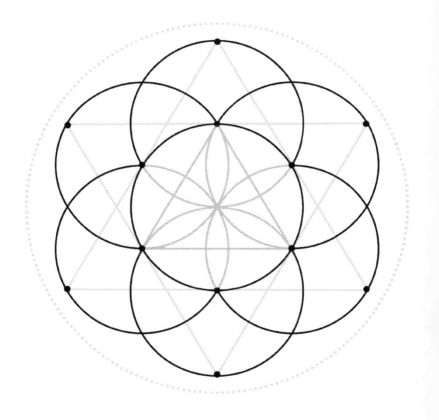

Each curveball covers:

THE LESSON
This is my life's journey

THE LEARNING
What you can learn from it

LISTEN IN
How you can use this in your
day to day life to support you

LIFE TOOLS
To help you dive in and
take a closer look

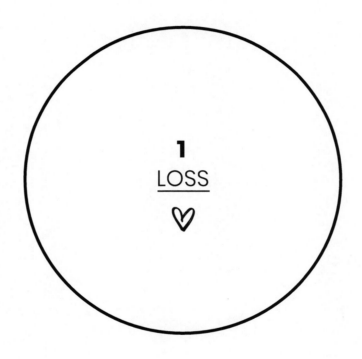

1
LOSS

"When I Look to the Sky" by Train

THE LESSON

THE WAKE UP CALL

It was the phone call that changed EVERYTHING.

It changed the trajectory of my whole life.

My family. My thoughts. My mindset. My future.

It was a cold dark October Halloween evening. I was lying awake stressing about the opening of a new hotel at Manchester Airport. I was the Assistant Director of Sales of a brand new five-star hotel and it was my responsibility to fill the hotels occupancy ready for opening.

I had been working tirelessly in a stuffy overheated porta cabin complete with suit, heels and hard hat for six months. Driving sales to get bums in beds ready for the opening while it was being built!

The next day was the grand opening. I was ready.

There was so much buzz around the hotel opening. All of the pomp and ceremony was due to commence. The 'opening team' had been fully briefed and everything was meticulously planned. I was beyond excited. The atmosphere was electric with the anticipation. Being part of a massive and super talented team, and to have all us revealing the biggest and best hotel there was in the area, gave me such a huge sense of self-worth and belonging.

It felt like the most important day of my life.

I had watched the hotel being built from the ground up and I was so proud. I had managed all of the sales campaigns to make sure we filled the hotel for the opening. This included daily show rounds, visits to hotel booking agents, corporate business presentations, travel agents tours, and I felt like I had made a difference to its potential success.

Picture the scene…

I was totally knackered yet very nervous, anxious and excited.

I had finished work for the day, kicked off my heels and snuggled on the sofa. I decided to stay in and chill with my bestie Gwen. We shared a few drinks and had a giggle before getting an early night. After all I needed my beauty sleep for the big day ahead of me.

In the early hours of the morning; 2 a.m. to be precise, and despite my excitement, to my own surprise, I managed to get to sleep and was dreaming away when the phone rang.

You know the type where it's ringing in your dream but it's actually ringing in reality…

It woke me with a start.

I was puzzled and I lay there wondering who on earth it could be calling at such an ungodly hour.

Do they not know I have the biggest day of my life happening in a few hours?

I could hear Gwen on the phone.

I scrambled out of bed in the dark just as she appeared at my bedroom door. She was as white as a ghost. I will never forget that look on her face and nothing could have prepared me for what she said next.

"Your Mum has had an asthma attack… and she has died."

My Mum. My best friend and my absolute world.

Had gone.

I think my heart actually stopped for a brief moment.

.
.
.
.
.

I had only spoken to her earlier that day. She had wished me good luck with the opening and she was so proud of my achievement.

My beautiful Mum, gone. At only fifty-four years of age.

She had so many plans for her future. So many places she still wanted to go and visit. Things yet to achieve. And now... just nothing

.
.
.
.
.

I couldn't comprehend what was happening.

I was numb. The news rocked me to my very core.

This happened when I was twenty-four years old.

As I tried to come to terms with my loss I counted my blessings that I had such a loving family around me. But I still felt like my world had fallen apart.

Crumbled to the very core.

I was frozen, as if my life was on hold.

It felt like my whole life tilted on its axis. Everything was moving around me but I was staying still. I was truly lost and broken.

I felt my heart shatter into a gazillion shards.

I was completely and utterly devastated.

Lost.

My mind couldn't process anything

I was agitated; numb and distracted all at the same time.

I couldn't even listen to music on the radio. I think all I managed was Classic FM, and I wanted to shout at people I saw, to tell them to be kind to their mums as they never knew when they would be taken away from them.

If you have loved and lost, you will know.

GRIEF AFFECTS US ALL IN SO MANY DIFFERENT WAYS.

Grieving is a natural response when we experience the death of someone close to us. Most people do not realise that grief is also a normal reaction when we suffer other types of losses in our lives too.

THE LEARNING

GRIEF IS NATURAL

- Loss of a parent, loved one, friend, relative
- Loss of a pet
- Loss of a job
- Loss of friendship
- Loss of health
- Loss of financial stability
- Loss of relationship, divorce or break up.

The process of grieving actually begins before we are fully aware that the loss has occurred. The shock waves created by life changes can cause emotional upheaval and lead to stress, anxiety and depression.

Trust me, I know this myself and if you have ever experienced this, you will too.

Quite often we will feel extremely afraid and insecure with the unfamiliarity and uncertainty brought about by change. This fear triggers strong emotions which can manifest themselves in ways that are both frightening and unpredictable.

A combination of anger, irritability, anxiety, sheer hopelessness, not wanting to speak, not knowing what to do. Utter devastation and the inability to cope can often lead to alcohol or drugs, which can, in turn, result in thoughts of self-harm or suicide

Coping with grief at any level can be complex. We are all individual and there are many ways in which we grieve.

When we experience grief it comes in different waves.

In order to understand what happens during the waves of grief, it is helpful to know the five phases that make up the response to loss.

There is a five phase cycle developed by Kubler Ross. However, please remember, not everyone experiences all five waves; you may navigate these quickly or get stuck on one for longer than someone else. It's a personal journey and varies from person to person.

Denial > Anger > Bargaining > Depression > Acceptance

THE CYCLE OF GRIEF

Kubler Ross's grief cycle, helps us consciously understand what happens when we experience grief.

I believe this grief cycle applies through any loss in life and how we process it.

When we experience loss, we wonder if the pain will ever go away. The scale of it can be unbearable and it can stir up a tsunami of emotions including sadness, anger, frustration, overwhelm and confusion.

Denial

Denial helps us reduce the overwhelming pain of loss. Our reality of what we knew before is no longer real and therefore we enter a period of disbelief. It can take our mind some time to shift to a new reality. At this stage it is difficult to see how we might move forward with our life because we haven't accepted what has happened and therefore can't process it.

Painful information running through our brain plays the main role here. It's the part that makes it difficult for us to process and then denial attempts to slow this processing down, so we can take it one step at a time. It allows us the time to absorb what is happening in our world.

Anger

It is perfectly normal and understandable to be angry when we experience loss, because we are trying to adjust to a new reality and likely to experience extreme discomfort.

Outwardly anger can also be perceived by others that you are unapproachable in the very moments you want comfort, connection and reassurance leaving you feeling isolated and alone.

Bargaining

The feeling of helplessness at this stage can cause you to react in a process known as bargaining. The process when everything feels so out of control we turn to something out of our control for change. This is where we can often inflict the questioning on ourselves and others...

The list goes on.

Depression

When our emotions start to calm down, reality starts to set in and we can no longer question and blame (bargain) as we realise there are no choices or changes that can be made. This is where a huge sense of sadness can ensue and we might find we are less sociable; retreating into our self or not wanting to talk.

This is a very natural stage of grief or loss and dealing with depression after the loss can feel very isolating. It is always important to seek help, there are lots of organizations that can help you.

You will find a list of resources on my website:
www.iamnaomivictoria.com/resources

Acceptance

When you arrive at a place of acceptance, it is not that we no longer feel the pain and just accept it. What it means is we are no longer resisting what has happened. We are aware of our reality and we are no longer trying to fight to make it something different.

Whilst sadness and regret can still be felt, the survival tactics of denial, bargaining and anger may become more subdued. Although this implies that we will work through the waves and reach closure, and while this may be possible with some losses in life, I personally believe, particularly where grief and more impactful losses are experienced, the cycle is exactly that.

We all grieve differently, and we may or may not go through all the stages. The lines can become blurred and sometimes we may move through a few and then back again. We are all individuals and how much time we spend in each phase will also differ to arrive at a place of acceptance. Depending on the loss, it may take days, months or even years.

We will heal and rebuild ourselves but our life will have changes.

I also believe that our grief cycle can get triggered during subsequent loss. E.g. the end of a relationship may trigger the grief felt for a loved one due to the emotions attached to that moment.

WHEN YOU ARE EXPERIENCING LOSS...

LISTEN IN

THE WAVES OF LOSS

Whatever time and whatever order this happens, know that it is perfectly normal.

Your pain is unique to you. It is ok to take the time you need, and it is more than okay to remove any expectation of how you should be. This is your process. Your loss and your grief.

Understanding the cycle exists, may help you identify and try to make sense of all that panic you feel and the white noise that loss stirs up.

WHEN YOU ARE EXPERIENCING LOSS

Loss can create a whirlpool within yet there are ways to deal with it and getting help and support is key.

1. Do you feel lonely?
It is completely normal to feel a sense of loneliness. Loss is a very individual thing, even if many people are affected by the same loss. If you are feeling lost, please reach out and get some help. Talk to friends and family or reach out to support groups or help lines (detailed in my resources section).

2. Who are you spending time with?
Choose your company. Be with people who have empathy and understanding with what you are going through. Connect with someone that will have the ability to hold space for you and not burden you further with their problems. If you don't know anyone, reach out to an organization or group.

3. Are you looking after YOU?
Be kind to yourself. It's totally ok not to be ok. Accept that you need time and you don't need to hold it all together.

4. Are you getting enough rest?
Rest and take your time. Loss can affect your emotional and physical well-being. It's important to stop and rest as much as you can.

5. Grab your internal surfboard and hold on to hope

Ride the waves. Emotions can hit like a tsunami at times. Release and accept that these waves of emotions, are perfectly normal. Often your thoughts can feel out of control. It is important to trust during these times and to practice self-care. Mindfulness, meditation, regular sleep; exercise and eating healthy food are just some of the ways to help you stay in balance. There are tools to help you in the Tools for Life Section.

6. Do you have a routine?

Having a daily routine allows you to try and keep your head together and manage overwhelm. Getting up and going to bed at the same time daily; making a brew; walking. Anything you can do to try and keep a routine.

7. Are you watching the clock?

Baby steps. You are not superhuman. Lots of people make judgements and may expect that you will bounce back in their defined period of time, however, in reality this is not the case. We are all unique. Go at your own pace and ignore others expectations of time.

8. What do you need? Right at this moment?

Inner need. Ask yourself what you need right now? Often for me it is a cuppa and a big blanket but it may be a walk by water or a snuggle with the dog or a visit to a friend.

9. Just breath...

Inhale and exhale. Breathe out fear and breathe in trust and know as scary as it is right now, it will pass.

JUST

Breathe

FINDING COMFORT

One of the ways I found comfort during my grief was by carrying something either sentimental or relevant with me at all times.

In the early days, after I lost my mum, it was a scarf of hers, I wore it to her funeral and kept it around me all the time. I still have it now although I don't wear it anymore. I also carried a heart in my purse as a reminder that she was always with me.

I have used tokens throughout my life since. These little tokens are reminders that it will pass, and whatever you are feeling right now will get easier. I promise.

the waves...

LIFE TOOLS

MORE LIFE TOOLS TO HELP YOU RIDE THE WAVES OF LOSS

EARTH
Page 197

 GROUNDING

 NURTURING NATURE

 MEDITATION

 CRYSTALS

AIR
Page 209

 LET GO

 JUST BREATHE

LOVE
Page 217

 SELF CARE RITUALS

SPACE
Page 245

 EFT

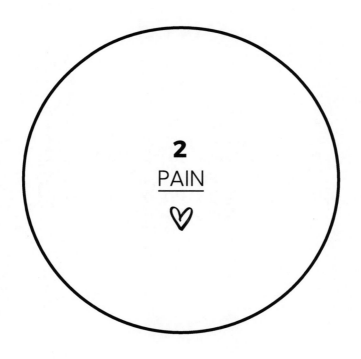

2

<u>PAIN</u>

"A Million Dreams" by The Greatest Showman

"Pain Changes everything,
but so does healing from it."

THE LESSON

PAIN CHANGES EVERYTHING

It was only a couple of weeks after I lost my mum, that I was pressurised to return to work. My head still in pieces and my heart torn apart. I tried my best to function, but everything had changed.

I just couldn't settle.

After a few months I decided I needed a change. I was head-hunted by another hotel company with a substantial increase in money and a promotion to National Accounts Manager. At first everything seemed great. The freedom of the road and zooming down the motorway with my tunes on full blast in my little company car. Travelling up to Scotland and down to London. It was a great distraction, but I soon got weary.

I would leave home on a Sunday evening, schlep around all week and not return home until late on Friday. The long days and nights away soon took their toll.

I was unhappy. I missed my family.

I couldn't work out where my life was going or what I actually wanted to do. I felt really lost inside. Losing my mum also showed me that life was just too short and I felt this niggle inside; something had to change.

One night I was sitting in a hotel room all alone in Scotland, reflecting on life, thinking about how much I missed my family.

I always carried a picture of my mum in a little heart frame in my purse. I sat on the bed and held it in my hand and sobbed. I missed her so much.

There was a weird indoor lagoon in the hotel I was staying at. The windows faced towards it.

The lagoon was like a dark, mystical cave with twinkling lights, and a soft murmur of running water never went away. It was pretty magical, although a little eerie when you are in your twenties on your own, in a hotel room that has a door into a dark lagoon.

But it was here I had my light bulb moment!

I no longer wanted to be away from my family.

I wanted to be at home with the ones I love.

What was I even doing with my life?

I wanted to achieve something special.

I wanted change.

NOW!

CREATING THE CHANGE

In my role as National Accounts Manager, I dealt with big and small organisations. I met hotel booking agents that had set themselves up in spare rooms, kitchen tables and garages. They all seemed happy and successful. They didn't have to schlep up and down the country or be away from their families.

I lay awake that entire night.

I had my very own eureka moment.

I could set up my own business!

But could I actually do this?

Every single scenario raced through my head. Self-doubt, excitement, fear and overwhelm. However, at sunrise, I had decided I could open my own business as a hotel booking agent.

I told myself, "I CAN TOTALLY DO THIS,"

"New Beginnings are often disguised as painful endings."
Lao Tzu

I spent the following days and weeks in a daydream thinking of all the things I could do and achieve. Then I would feel sick to my stomach and question myself constantly, could I really do this?

If you are self-employed or you have left a job or been for an interview that you never thought you would get, you will know the feeling!

I was petrified. The thought of leaving a full-time well-paid job to go it alone was a seriously scary thought. I still remember the sleepless nights and the what if's?

What if I fail?

What if I can't pay the mortgage?

What if I'm not good enough?

What if I don't have enough money to buy a car?

What if no one likes me?

What if I run out of money?

I was absolutely riddled with self-doubt.

I spent days creating all kinds of plans, business plans, marketing schedules, forecasts and sales targets (and started to wish I had listened more in my accountancy lessons at university).

I drew out logos; colour schemes; designed and dreamed about what the website would look like. Brain downloaded names and domain names. I was so excited.

- Then I would go into panic mode.
- What if everyone thought this was a really stupid idea?
- What if they laughed at me?
- What if they thought I was just ridiculous?

FEELING THE FEAR

Although I was super excited. I was also full of fear. I had no idea how to run a business and the prospect of not having a wage petrified me. I think more than anything I was fearful of failing.

I decided to have a meeting with my Dad. I have always really admired my Dad although we didn't live together when I was growing up, I used to love going to see him and he inspired me hugely in life.

Self-made, my father was a very successful business man and I always respected his opinion.

I put my big girl knickers on and ran the idea by him, which to me at the time was a bit like getting approval from the *Dragon's Den* panel or Richard Branson. I knew he would want to see a business plan, and it was highly likely that he would think it was another one of my quirky hair brained ideas. I've had a few in the past!

Armed with all my business plans and a thousand thoughts running through my head, I sat down with him over lunch. I soon picked up the courage to present my idea.

He would roll his eyes and say it was a ridiculous suggestion and I could just stay in employment, right?

My negative mind chatter was in overdrive. Expecting the worst. Expecting him to tell me my idea was just a pipe-dream.

He will say no.
Don't even bother asking him.
Who are you?
A business owner? Now, that is laughable.

Then came the pause. My chance to speak up. And before I knew it, I shared my idea with him.

I took a deep breath whilst crossing my fingers under the table.

After I told him my idea, he surprised me by sharing his own entrepreneurial dreams, but had chosen the corporate path instead.

Although he never lived out his dream to own his own business, he was an extremely successful businessman and happy with his career path.

What he said next, I will never forget...

What the actual hell?!

Well, this really means I'm doing this then! I had his approval.

I actually skipped back to my car that day and my entrepreneurial journey began.

It now makes me laugh that I actually needed my dad's approval but that's something we will come back to later on.

Although 'the keeping me safe part of me', was kind of hoping he would say it was a stupid idea.

Part of me was trying to stay small.

But that never happened.

So I went for it!

WHAT SCARES YOU THE MOST?

Is there something that you are feeling fearful of right now?

Ask yourself...

- What's the worst that could happen?
- What if I fail?
- Then ask yourself... BUT what if I fly?

And ALWAYS go with the latter. These days I don't really believe in failure. Failure is a lesson that redirects you to something else. It's not a bad thing. It's actually a great thing.

"What if I fail?
Oh, but my darling but
what if you fly?"
Erin Hanson

I DID IT...

THE PLAN

I did it...

On 1 January 2000, I opened my first business.

I had spent months searching for an office. I found a small space with a store; the rent was reasonable, and I took to work renovating it and making it mine. I decided to start as I meant to go on.

Setting my stall out.

I meant business.

I recruited staff; bought computers and a server; spent a ton of time at IKEA choosing my desk and my Dad helped me to get a car so I could get out on the road and see clients.

Within a few weeks I was ready.

I had offices, a website and a team of staff. I had brochures printed and sent out mailshots.

So, the sales would just come, right?

WRONG!

I tried everything. Telesales, mailshots, cold calling, door-to-door marketing, even those sticky blob things with a promotional message in an attempt to grab people's attention.

Remember, we are going back, way before the days of social media. Back then, we used to connect to people we knew via the telephone, fax (yeah, I said fax) or Friends Reunited. Remember that? The days were long; the sales were bleak and the bank balance reflected that.

It was pitiful.

Within twelve months I had gone from the fear of failure to the excitement of bringing it all to life; to sheer panic that I was going to lose it all before I had really even started.

The overheads, the pressure of staff and wages it all came crashing in.

I realised that no amount of business planning was going to help me at this point. In fact they felt like a load of bollocks and told me nothing about real life, relationships and how it was actually going to be in reality.

"If the plan doesn't work change the plan not the goal."

My dad was amazing and supported me in ways I can't even begin to explain.

He made me report to him and he would, in turn, give me one of his pep talks. It would drive me and catapult me into action and I would go back to building relationships and making sales.

I would do ANYTHING to make this work. It just had to.

I WAS NOT GOING TO FAIL!

Failure wasn't an option.

My dad spent days showing me how to do my own accounts. I learned later in life that I wasn't born to be an accountant. No matter how many hours he spent with me, it was all in vain because none of it actually went in to my brain.

I am definitely right-brained. I am more of a creative and intuitive thinker and the sequencing and mathematical left-brained task of accounts does not suit me at all. It didn't back then, and it still doesn't now.

DAYS BEFORE GOOGLE

Back in those days, working online meant dialling up by a phone line. Remember all that annoying crackly noise? Yup, me too.

I spent days and weeks, researching prospects and contacts. Believe me, using dial up was a painstakingly long process.

We soon invested in a fancy whizzy ISDN line which saved us a tonne of time.

I remember the day my dad rang me to tell me there was this great new thing called Google.

I don't remember how we coped pre-Google. Do you?

As the internet took off so did my business and the hard work eventually paid off.

The phones started to ring, the emails pinged and the clients and contracts came.

YES.

Systems saved my life. Or at least they saved my business.

Profits increased and the growth continued. I was now pitching for large contracts with some really big agencies. I bought my first ever brand new car. Moved into my new apartment.

I genuinely thought I was living the dream.

My business was financially successful.

I moved into my new apartment. The success was paying off and the bank balance was blooming.

So everything was now going to 'plan' at work, but what about me?

I felt really lonely inside. It was time to look at my own life. All of it.

I took time to focus on my Life Plan. Something I hadn't done since I started the business.

Several months later, I finally found my new love. I met my future husband. We moved in together and this gave me the stability I was so desperately seeking. With stability came reflection and I dreamed about what I really wanted to do next. While I had created success, I spent long hours in a stuffy office and had started to dislike a lot of the work.

Another Naomi light bulb moment.

"I will open a shop."

Six months later and in true Naomi style, I achieved my goal and opened a shop.

lessons...

THE LEARNING

Do

- Use Google. It's the biggest search engine in the world.
- Create a Life Plan but remember it shouldn't be set it stone, we have to be flexible when the time comes. We'll get to that next.
- Believe in yourself.
- Follow your dreams.
- Believe that you are good enough and anything is possible.
- Carry out a life stock take (we'll get to that in Listen In next).

Don't

- Let your dreams and excitement mask the small print.
- Always listen to your dad's advice (you may not ever really want to be an accountant #givingyoupermission).
- Spend all your time focussing on business plans or money goals. Yes while they are great to have, a realistic and positive mindset will be more useful.
- Worry about what other people think.
- Dwell on the bad days. Take time out and remember tomorrow is another day!
- If something isn't working, don't panic, just change the plan.

LEFT | RIGHT

ANALYSIS

MATHS

IDEA

LOGIC

FACTS

REASON

LANGUAGE

SEQUENCING

ARTS

MUSIC

EMOTIONS

IMAGINATION

COLOURS

CREATIVITY

INTUITION

DREAMS

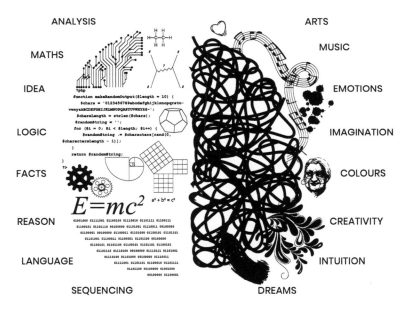

YOUR BRAIN

I mentioned earlier that I am right-brained. Knowing if you are left-brained or right-brained MATTERS.

In life and business it's good to identify our strengths and weaknesses.

You see, the theory goes that we are either left-brained or right-brained, meaning one side of our brain is more dominant than the other.

Left brain theory is known to be more logical, linear, sequential, analytical and objective whereas right brain theory is more holistic, creative, emotional, intuitive and subjective.

Which are you?

CREATING PLANS

Earlier I referred to business plans as being bollocks. This is true if you don't fully align the plan with your actual business and you restrict any change or flow. In business and life, there is absolutely no point in creating a document shoving it in a file and never revisiting it.

I do, however, believe that having a framework around which to work is useful in both work and life.

1. Embrace the new you

Making life changes can feel scary. That's why lots of people put it off for as long as possible. But think about this. When was the last time anything worth doing was easy? If you want to make positive changes in your life, accept that things won't always remain exactly the same, and the new you may actually turn out to feel more amazing than the current you.

2. Make goals relevant to you

Once you know what to change and you start to feel those life-changing butterflies fluttering around in your stomach, it's time to sit down and develop a plan. Ask yourself, where do I want to be by the end of this year? Make it quantifiable, do you want to lose weight or quit smoking by a certain date? These goals are good for keeping yourself accountable but make sure you know why. If they don't mean anything to you personally, it will be harder to stay motivated.

3. Be mindful throughout the change

Keep checking in with yourself. Ask yourself how you are feeling and what this change is going to do for you.

4. Give yourself credit

The term 'life change' can sometimes feel overwhelming. This means that instead of focusing on all the life changes you've made in recent months, pick one life change that has been especially significant for you and give yourself credit for working towards achieving it. It doesn't have to be an enormous life change either we should acknowledge even minor life changes since they will begin to add up over time.

5. Change is a process

Positive life changes take time and patience. The process can challenge you, but once you see your life change come to life, it will become worth every single struggle and obstacle that gets thrown your way. The most important step towards making life changes is getting started with deciding and making one small step today.

DO YOU HAVE A PLAN FOR YOUR LIFE?

LISTEN IN

THE LIFE PLAN

Do you know where you are heading and how you are going to get there?

"A dream without a plan is just a dream."

Plans change; curve balls come in; we grow; we evolve; we change; we are not a formalised document stuck in a file; life simply doesn't work that way.

So how can you create change and a life plan that will work for you?

TAKING STOCK

Well first up I would take stock of where you are currently at.

Take yourself out on a date, yep, like a real live date.
Go to your favourite place. Sit by the sea; go to a restaurant; visit a coffee shop; take a walk in the park.
Take a notebook with you and grab a cuppa.
Have a think about where you are in your life.
Write it down, document how you are feeling and what your life actually looks and feels like RIGHT NOW in this very moment.

- Are you frustrated and overwhelmed?

- Are you feeling lost and alone?

- Are you happy and grateful?

- Do you want more out of your life?

- Are you content?

- Do you feel stressed?

- Are you feeling peaceful?

- Do you feel balanced?

- Do you want more money?

- Do you want more time to spend with the kids?

- Do you want to spend more time on your own?

It's time to be completely honest with yourself.

Completely and utterly empty your head of where you are at. I call this my brain dump.

Now, read everything back and ask yourself...

- What needs to stay?

- What needs to go?

- What do you want more of?

- What do you need to release?

Assess each area of your life, your career or business, family and friends. Relationships, your home, hobbies and leisure and personal growth.

Break it all down and ask yourself...

- What do I want my life to actually look like?
- Does it look like it does now? If not, what would I like to change?

This is **NOT** an exercise to write a big long list. Or dwelling on what you don't have right now. This is not a pity party. This is giving you the opportunity to look at every aspect of your life. To help you celebrate how far you have come.

And it also gives you the chance to dream. To think about goals you wish to achieve. Then bathe in appreciation for all you have today in the here and now. This is your starting point. Your new perspective.

Where would you like to travel to? I'm not saying you need to set sail straight away, but dreaming is exciting. Maybe then you would start planning an itinerary and set your navigation to see how long the journey would take you (that would be the start of the planning process).

You can create a life plan any way you want to. You could doodle it in a book, you could type it up and create it digitally or you could record a voice memo. Whatever works for you.

But the one thing I do recommend is you get it out of your head and start to realise that you actually have a plan and dreams. I've shared some life planning tools in the next section to help you.

freedom...

LIFE TOOLS
TO HELP YOU NAVIGATE LIFE AND FIND FREEDOM

WATER
Page 225

 SELF DISCOVERY

 VISUALISATION

 DESIGN YOUR DREAM

 YOUR VISION BOARD

SOUND
Page 237

 MUSIC AND MOVEMENT

FIRE
Page 257

 LIGHTING UP YOUR LIFE

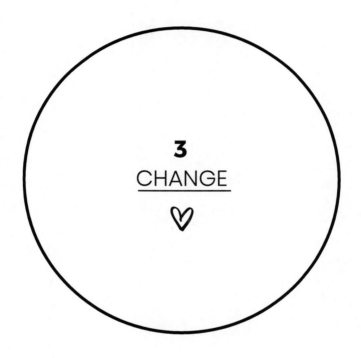

3
CHANGE

"Beyond the Sea" by Robbie Williams

THE LESSON

TRIALS, TRIBULATIONS & TRIBUNALS

It had always been a big dream of mine to be an interior designer.

There was a small interior design shop near my house as I was growing up, right next to the sweet shop I adored. I used to look into the window and wonder if one day this could be mine.

As much as I tried and as creative as I am, I was never good enough at art.

I looked at the qualifications required for an Interior Design Degree. You guessed it, art. Instead I opted to train as a chef and channel my creative flair there instead.

My dreams of interior design were quashed at an early age, however, they never really left me.

At the age of thirty I was still holding on to that dream of opening a shop and I knew then I had to do something about it. A little voice in my head told me...

"Open the shop, Naomi. Open it. Do it. Do it. You could open an interiors shop, you love interiors."

GENIUS. I thought. I could do it, right?

I spent weeks looking around shops for rent. Scoping out the best areas, the locations, foot traffic.

It was a whole new world to me and most of the lease holders wanted five to ten year lease contract commitments. In addition, the rent required plus the deposits were astronomical.

Remember the interior design shop I loved as a little girl? One day it just so happened to come up for let. It was sitting waiting for me.

That shop had my name on it.

But could it really be that I could open my very own shop there?

Without hesitation, I arranged a viewing and my dad came along to view it with me. Again, I trust him implicitly and if he said it was a go-er then I knew I was on to a good thing.

As soon my foot stepped over that door threshold, I fell in love with it.

In my true Dad style, he stepped in with his practical head on, "Naomi it's too small. Think about sales per square foot, the traffic, the parking..."

I listened to his advice. I took it all on board and knew he was right. It was too small and it just wasn't meant to be.

But I didn't give up. A few weeks later I finally found the one.

It was BIG. It had three floors with an outdoor balcony on the second floor and I knew that it had so much potential.

It felt expansive.

Nestled between a small row of shops with parking outside and offices space on the top floor. It had a store room which would be separate office for me. I could really make this suit all of my business needs. It felt perfect.

I vividly remember the day I got the keys. When I arrived at the shop reality hit.

It was just an empty shell. There was so much work to do.

Complete decoration across all three floors was required. It needed new flooring, a service counter, shelving, signage, shutters, security and stock, we needed so much stock to fill every square inch of the place.

from**house**to**home**

I worked twenty four seven. I didn't sleep for weeks. I was living on the buzz of it all. Thriving and surviving on it. I was so excited. After all, I was living my dream, right?

And nothing was left to chance. I ensured I ordered hard-wearing natural carpets for the floors to enhance their longevity and high foot traffic. Painting for hours on end. Cleaning the place from corner to corner. Floor planning. Stock buying. CCTV. Signage. You name it, we did it.

In just four short weeks, together, as a family and with help of my friends too, we transformed the place.

Then the stock arrived. Lots of stock. Boxes and boxes of the stuff. Crates of goods to fill my HUGE shop. Sofas, cabinets, tables, pictures, mirrors, and that was just the start. We had over one thousand stock lines of glassware, crockery, kitchen accessories, cushions, throws, candles, signs, fragrance, gifts, Christmas decorations... the list goes on.

Every single item required barcoding and pricing so we could set up the stock management system. I really hadn't prepared for the amount of work involved. But we did it.

Shelves up, glasses on, it was like a beautiful treasure trove. The shop was ready; shutters were fitted and the signage went up above the door.

'From House To Home' was born.

I stood back on the street and looked at the window.

I had actually achieved what I wanted. I had brought my dream to life.

I set about organising a grand opening, which was incredible. We had caterers providing champagne and canapés, the local media turned up in droves and the place was buzzing. The feedback we received was amazing.

I was so chuffed with myself. I went around mingling with everyone thinking, I should have done this years ago and also yay, cha ching! The till was ringing with sales. That sound was music to my ears and our first sales were realised.

In the background though, I was really struggling to manage both businesses because the hotel booking agency was still located in offices a few miles away and the shop was open all day.

So I made an even bigger decision. I simply couldn't run both businesses at the same time and decided to step away from the hotel booking agency to allow me to focus on my shop's success instead. It was where my true heart and passion lay.

I had a great team of staff at the shop led by me and while they worked certain shifts, I worked around the clock.

A few months after opening, I was getting married. The shop consumed so much of my time that I planned my whole wedding at the service counter in the shop, three weeks before I was due to get married, I still hadn't bought my wedding shoes!

Somehow we pulled it all together and had a beautiful day surrounded by my incredible family. My Dad walked me down the aisle and I felt on top of the world. The happiest I had ever been.

My husband and I had so many amazing plans for the future. We headed off to the Maldives on our honeymoon which was pure bliss. It really is the picture perfect paradise.

On our return, the shop had survived in my absence and life was really good. A few weeks later life got even better, I discovered I was pregnant.

BABY CHANGING

I was going to have a baby. Me. Naomi. Going to be a mum.

I had dreamed of this moment all my life. I had wanted children since my early twenties and now it was actually happening.

Everything was falling into place. A booming business, an amazing husband, a beautiful home and a new bouncing baby.

Life couldn't get much better... But, they do say you have to experience the falls to appreciate the highs.

The next part of my journey was stressful and for legal reasons I won't provide details but the decision I made previously, to step away from my hotel booking agency, triggered an extremely stressful employment tribunal.

I was pregnant. I struggled through the whole process. I felt like I was getting attacked by the very people I had cared for and supported for years. The backlash of events was hard and the stress started to take its toll on my health.

Once again I went to my Dad for advice and he said, "Naomi, nothing is worth this stress for you and the baby. If you have to make settlement payments, let's just do it. What price can you actually put on your health?" He was right.

Thousands of pounds later, and an out of court settlement it all went away.

I'm a big believer in karma, not getting bitter and not wasting energy, so I turned my focus and energy into the shop and my pregnancy.

The shop was booming, it felt like home from home for me. I would walk in every morning and light candle on the counter it would smell of sumptuous chocolate and warm vanilla, the furniture ranges and accessories were seriously beautiful. My staff were amazing and as my bump got bigger, the workload grew more tiring too. My incredible team stepped in and helped.

The shop was always buzzing with people who required design advice, a service we offered. I would be running (or more wobbling) up and down the stairs pulling design ideas together. Displaying accessories around furniture with them, ensuring I created the right 'look and feel' the clients were looking for. We stocked everything and more often than not, they would buy the lot. I really was in my element.

Baby Molly arrived into the world and I had never loved anyone more. I stared at her all day and night, but I was back in the shop after just three days (if you have ever watched *Brittas Empire*, the scene with the baby under the desk) it was similar to that with my baby behind the counter and me juggling to serve customers. But none of it bothered me. This was my life. I was thriving and I loved every single minute of it.

The days were long. I once again juggled orders, packed boxes, fed Molly, and grabbed snippets of time while she was asleep and trundling off to the warehouse to source stock.

The pressure I began to feel inside grew and became immense.

Suddenly I didn't feel so happy. I wanted to be, but I didn't feel it. I also didn't feel well in myself. I put a lot of it down to stress, but the distraction of work, the focus of driving sales gave me the sense of feeling happy. It made me feel successful. It gave me my sense of self-worth. It made me feel alive and empowered.

A year later Molly was learning to walk (a little later than average) but she was up and about. My sister one day noticed that there seemed to be a problem with her leg, I took her off to the hospital and it wasn't long before we got the devastating diagnosis. She had hip dysplasia. Something that hadn't been identified during her hip checks. The prognosis wasn't good. Major surgery and a full body cast.

I was devastated. My baby was going to need surgery.

It was complex surgery. Hours of surgery on my baby girl. They wanted to delay the surgery until Molly was two years old and we needed to wait another four months. The wait was excruciating for me. Apprehension built. The worry. It all felt too much.

During that time I was admitted to hospital. My health had deteriorated and I needed to stay in for a week for tests as the doctors weren't quite sure what was wrong with me. The whole episode was hideous. Worrying about Molly and wondering what was wrong with me. Being away from my baby girl. Leaving the business in the safe hands of my staff. I trusted them but, I was so hands on in the business that it was also my baby.

I finally received my diagnosis and was admitted for surgery.

With a six-week recovery time for myself, I was cutting it fine in being able to care for Molly, who was due for surgery too. I knew I had to be healthy enough to care for her, so I bolstered all of my mental strength to make that happen.

At that time the demise of the high street began. Luck did not appear to be on my side.

The shop sales were bleak and the beautiful row of shops that my own shop sat amongst became more like a derelict shell of empty units. Dozens of 'To Let' signs went up every day. Foot fall declined and I made a life changing decision to move all of my stock from a physical shop and take it online.

It was a tough lesson as I had signed a ten-year lease which was complex to navigate.

I remember coming out of hospital and my husband passing me parcels on the sofa to wrap as I couldn't afford to take the time off or pay anyone to help me and I had no other choice.

Then Molly went in for her surgery. Five and a half hours of waiting. It felt much longer.

Molly needed care twenty four seven.

She was incredible. She never complained or cried. She just embraced the situation, the cast weighed over a stone and she even managed to learn to crawl in it. She's one remarkable girl. One very resilient young lady and an absolute inspiration.

I CAN BE CHANGED WHAT HAPPENS TO ME. BUT I REFUSE TO BE REDUCED BY IT.
MAYA ANGELOU

CHANGE IS INEVITABLE AT ALL STAGES THROUGHOUT OUR LIFE. CAN YOU SEE ALL THE UPS AND DOWNS IN THIS CHAPTER OF MY LIFE?

THE LEARNING

COPING WITH CHANGE & BUILDING RESILIENCE

Some changes are easier to accept than others, for example planned changes; growing up and the changes of seasons. Significant or unexpected change is often far more challenging.

I call them curveballs. So let's take a look at what actually happens when they come and land themselves in our life.

INITIAL SHOCK

Any change can have a physical effect on us and when an unexpected change comes into our life adrenaline kicks in. Our body has to react to the information received and sends us into a flight or fight response which acts as a form of protection. It feels like we are under threat and therefore there is an instant need to run for the hills and make it go away or stand your ground and fight the battle.

"This too shall pass."

This tends to pass fairly quickly and once things start to sink in, we move into...

Resistance to Change
Not wanting to accept what is happening. Denial. Just wanting things back as they were; desperately wanting to reverse time and pretend this just isn't happening to you.

Frustration/Overwhelm
As we start to process the curveball that we have been delivered and realise another outcome (i.e. turning back time) is not possible, it can feel like we have nowhere to go with our emotions. A feel of desperation and hopelessness may start to set in.

Powerless
We sit within a void we can't go back and we are not ready to move forwards. At this stage it is super important to gather support around you to help and enable you to move into...

Coping
The realisation that we need to find a way forward. Looking at what options are available to us. This support will help guide you into...

Acceptance
Where you can move on with your life, where calmer waters are found and you can start to discover growth and see a future.

At every stage of uncertainty and change, you can anchor into knowing that this too shall pass.

We cannot always control the circumstances around us but we can control how we react to them.

"Resilience is not about being resilient to everything in life, it's about finding your own resilience when faced with the obstacles that come along in life."

RESILIENCE & STRENGTH

Resilience is about having an inner strength that allows you to be strong in the face of challenges.

It's about how you bounce back from adversity. How you can develop and use your inner strength and power to rise above difficult situations.

It is about how you respond to change, rather than why the change actually happened. It's knowing what your aims are, even when faced with challenges or adversity and being able to remain focused on what you want to achieve in life rather than becoming overwhelmed by the obstacles that you face.

It is being able to recognise your own inner potential. Often in times of crisis and difficulty and establishing a strong sense of self-belief and self-esteem, will keep you going even when things don't go according to plan.

RESILIENCE IS SOMETHING WE HAVE TO FIND WITHIN OURSELVES.

LISTEN IN

The first step toward creating your own resilience is to assess where you currently stand and what areas you need to work on.

Take a moment to consider the people who have become resilient in your life. It's likely that you'll notice that resilience is an ongoing process—a journey rather than a destination.

THE CHANGE CURVEBALL

Have you experienced any curveballs lately?

How did you cope?

How did you respond?

It can all look a little like this...

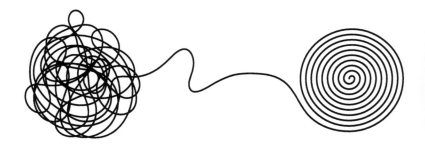

But there are ways which we can take control of uncertainty and actually spiral INTO control.

Do you think you could improve your overall resilience?

If so, it's time to think about your own coping curveball of change so you can cope better with difficult situations.

Choice
When the change is out of control, how can you control your own actions?

You can choose to dramatise it and be the victim.

Or you can choose to accept what is happening and focus on using all of your energy to navigate the storm.

Care
How can you take care of yourself during what may seem like a tsunami at the time?

Think about an oxygen mask and a life jacket, when you step on to a flight. The crew tell you to put your oxygen mask on first so you breathe, to help yourself before you can help others. The same applies to your life jacket.

Taking care of **you** during a crisis or uncertainty is no different and super important.

What things could you do to look after yourself at this time?

What would your life buoy look like? Think of it like a tool box.

To give you an idea of what's in my life buoy...

No alcohol

Time to breathe

Early nights

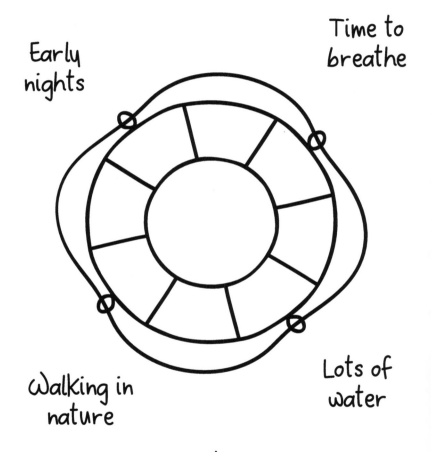

Lots of water

Walking in nature

Healthy meals

What's in your life buoy?

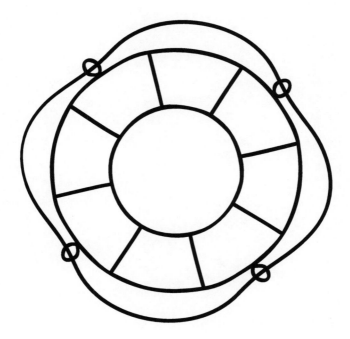

Knowledge
Is there anything you could research? Is there any knowledge you can gain to get the facts about a situation that will allow you to put it into some form of perspective instead of allowing the thoughts to spiral out of control in your head?

Gratitude
Focus on the good stuff. This can seem really counter intuitive during the tidal waves of unexpected change or trauma but getting grounded and focussing on gratitude really helps you anchor yourself to stop the rocky waters around you, while you navigate yourself to calmer waters.

Resilience is not automatic; we can develop it. It's an ongoing process, so don't get discouraged if you hit snags along the way to increased resilience.

Instead, view these ideas as opportunities for growth, rather than a to do list.

change...

LIFE TOOLS

TO HELP YOU NAVIGATE CHANGE

EARTH
Page 197

 NURTURING NATURE

 MINDFULNESS

 MEDITATION

AIR
Page 209

 YOUR BUBBLE

LOVE
Page 217

 SELF CARE RITUALS

FIRE
Page 257

 SUNSHINE OF GRATITUDE

 IGNITING INTENTION WITH AFFIRMATIONS

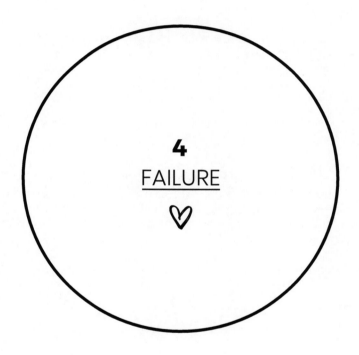

4

<u>FAILURE</u>

"Maybe Tomorrow" by Stereophonics

THE LESSON

DARING TO GROW

Molly started to walk. Yep, actually on two legs, moving and everything. It was a joyous day.

A day filled with hope and possibility.

To see her stand independently at age four was a feeling I will never forget. She had come such a long way and it was a massive inspiration to witness.

Her resilience and strength at such a young age was incredible.

Now she had her new-found independence, she started nursery part-time and loved it.

And business was booming again.

Stock lines sold out and I was continuously thinking about new product ranges, testing the market and monitoring the trends. I was absolutely determined to make an amazing life for myself and my family.

And to make it even more amazing I discovered I was pregnant again.

Beautiful little Ruby arrived into our world. I really felt that my life was truly complete.

However, I was juggling life like crazy running the business; hold down a house, be a wife, and be a mum. 'Me time' had become a distant memory.

I kept on working. Kept on being busy. One day when I was searching for new stocklines for the shop, I discovered rattan garden furniture. You know the stuff that you can leave outside all year round? That stuff.

Well back then it wasn't really a thing. We all had teak garden furniture that we oiled year in year out.

I heard about this new type of furniture and jumped straight on it. I was lucky enough to find a contact in the UK that could supply me with some. So I ordered my first garden sofa set. It cost three hundred pounds which was a big risk for me. It was the most I had spent on a single item since having my shop.

I listed it on the website and guess what? It sold.

I had doubled my money and made three hundred in one sale. Woo hoo!

I was so excited about my first big item, so I ordered another and again, it sold. Then another and another and so it continued.

To hold my increasing stock, I rented a small storage unit just a few miles away from my house and my new furniture venture was born.

Orders flew in. Everyday. I needed more supply. More storage, more everything to manage the demand. It just kept expanding.

Before long I ordered my first full container of stock. I know right. ME? Ordering a container from China. I found it laughable. I couldn't believe I was actually doing it either.

Ten thousand pounds lighter. *Eeek*. It felt SO scary. Paying out that kind of money. I knew I had to make this work. I was still working from home, zooming to the storage unit every time we got a sale while juggling family life. It was crazy and wonderful all at once.

Our success drove a change. We knew it had to happen.

Ruby came to work with me, everyday. The unit I was renting was freezing and no place for a baby.

So I ordered myself a little summerhouse to work from at the front of the unit. This would become my office. Molly was at school by this time then Ruby started nursery not long after, and it really felt like my life was changing in big ways.

The next few years were bonkers.

I was literally working seven days a week, juggling being a mum, a wife and having a full-on busy business. My husband worked full time too and we barely saw anything of each other. It was manic. But I was making money. Really good money.

Within eighteen months the business had grown so much I didn't know what to do with the money. I had never had this much money in my whole life. I turned over my first million (well nearly it was £967,000 to be precise). We had grown financially as well as hiring staff. I had a team of eight and I felt really successful and so very proud of myself.

everything...

EVERYTHING TO EVERYONE

I had it all. My beautiful girls and the business I had always dreamed of, and money beyond belief. I felt so proud of the success I had achieved. But underneath all I was still unhappy. Things were not good at home in my personal life. My business was growing so fast I couldn't keep on top of it all. I was trying to be everything to everyone, mum, wife, boss.

Something had to give and it wasn't long before it took its toll on my relationships. Time with my girls suffered as did my health and my happiness.

Finally my marriage broke down.

The one thing I had always craved in life was a happy family unit. The stereotype idea of mum, dad and kids all sitting down for dinner together, Sunday roasts and holidays by the sea. And here I was breaking up my own family home. My head was like mashed potato, it felt like someone had put my head in a blender. It was all so jumbled up. I was juggling stress at work and now navigating a separation and divorce.

It felt like one thing after another and every year it felt like the treacle I was walking through got stickier and stickier.

But I kept on trudging.

My future had no certainty and there were so many times I struggled with anxiety. I felt lost and overwhelmed and didn't know what I was actually going to do or if I would actually get through it. But guess what?

Somehow, I did.

I then made a series of catastrophic mistakes. I lost control of the business. I messed up and made stupid decisions.

I wasn't focussed. I took risks in my personal life.

I moved out of my family home to live on my own with my girls. Let me tell you, it was not easy to navigate a house move with an infant and a toddler.

I was trying to juggle it all.

THE FIREFIGHTER

My business was in massive difficulty. I had huge amounts of stock that I had to store out of season due to a flooded summer season (not very handy when you are retailing garden furniture). I was advised to sell It all off out of season (to liquidate my stock) to recoup soaring storage costs.

When the weather improved, the orders started flooding in again, however, I didn't see the upturn with other well know brand names starting to stock the furniture. The factories couldn't produce enough stock and I couldn't fulfil the orders. The whole thing was crumbling around me and I soon found myself at crisis point.

I will never forget the day my Dad came to a meeting with me and my management accountants.

My Dad's words were, "Between us we have let Naomi down. She employed you to take care of the finances and oversee the business. She trusted in us all and you didn't do your jobs and I didn't see."

I just sat there, silent and broken.

My Dad was fighting my corner in a world I didn't understand.

Love you Dad.

For the next six months I was firefighting. Trying to hold everything together and keep afloat trying my very best to trade my way through it all. The stress was immense. I would sit night after night juggling figures whilst trying to be there for my girls too and holding my head in my hands wondering how on earth I was going to get through it all. At one point I was rushed into hospital with a suspected stroke.

Finally I had to stop and admit defeat. I had to step back and I made a decision to put the business into liquidation.

I had lost it all. I felt a complete failure. I felt responsible that people were going to lose their jobs. I owed people money. I wanted to hide away and never show my face again.

I was living alone with my girls. My business was gone and the bills just kept coming. I just couldn't keep up.

I immediately started to sell 'stuff' on eBay. I tried desperately to start again and I was just about keeping a roof over the girl's heads, but it wasn't enough.

Looking back, I wonder how I even managed to hold all this together and navigate these waters.

I knew that I needed to create change.
I knew I had to do something for the girls.

I remember my Dad telling me to go and get a proper job and after applying for loads and having just one interview it soon became apparent that I was unemployable. I think I had been self-employed that long and people said I was overqualified or would just say that I was going to take their ideas into my own business and couldn't comprehend why I would want to go back to corporate life.

My dad loaned me two hundred pounds to buy some food for the kids. I spent fifty on food the rest on new business cards to start up again. I was desperate and I just knew I had to do it for the girls. I needed to try, for them so I could keep a roof over their heads and to make sure that we could survive.

Digging really deep, I somehow found the strength to start again.

I set up a new business.

I had no self-confidence and no self-esteem, I felt so lost and alone but I was doing it, I was making it happen, I joined some local business networks and I managed to get clients and they started to pay. I was frantically grasping onto anything I could, trying to pay all the bills to keep it all afloat but the bills kept coming and soon it became all too much.

Picture the scene, I had been trying my best all day to keep a smiley face, trying to be brave for my girls. I bathed them and tucked them in to bed when there was a loud knock at the front door. I rushed down to answer it and there were two burly blokes dressed in black demanding my car keys.

Baliffs.

The girls heard commotion from upstairs and they came down. They were hysterical. "Mummy why are those men taking our car away." I choked back the tears and just about managed to hold it together to settle them back off to bed and as soon as they were asleep I literally sat huddled in a ball on the kitchen floor and sobbed.

Once again I felt like a complete failure.
I felt like I had failed as a wife.
I felt like I failed in my business and I felt like I failed as a mum.

I didn't sleep a wink that night and the next morning I couldn't even get the girls to school. Thankfully my friends rallied round and helped me.
I was now in full survival mode.

If you are experiencing financial difficulties, please get the help you need. There are some incredible charities out there that will help you.

THE LEARNING

NAVIGATING UNCERTAINTY

If you are dealing with uncertainty in your life right now, just like we all did during the lockdown and pandemic, my best advice would be, just stop where you are and take in a big breath and then breathe again...
just breathe and know and trust that change is possible.

This will pass and with belief and hope in your heart you will be able to navigate the storm.

Coping with uncertainty can be hard, and you may find yourself struggling to keep afloat through stormy waters. We often try to just cope, by shifting our attention away from things we don't like or want – such as thinking of something else, distracting ourselves and trying not to worry. But when faced with uncertainty, distraction isn't the answer. It's important to sit with and process the feelings.

No matter what happens, you'll have some fears whether things turn out positively or negatively.

The more you practise coping strategies, the better prepared you'll be to face up to future uncertainties and find coping techniques that really work for you.

Navigating uncertainty is a part of everyday life and by practising and by using the tools I have shared in the next section, you'll be able to approach uncertainty in a more proactive way that's healthier in the long run.

Learning new strategies can help reduce fears. But it isn't about trying to convince yourself that everything will work out perfectly or positive thinking when this isn't realistic.

Rather than telling yourself that everything will turn out fine no matter what happens, they teach us something important – by being prepared for the worst so we don't get caught off-guard if things do go wrong.

It's important to remember that they are coping strategies rather than magic wands.

Think of it like you are sitting in a boat and rowing whilst embracing the journey to unknown shores, we can work out in our heads all the different scenarios, but ultimately, we need to also hold and trust the journey.

There was a great book I read during my divorce by Susan Jeffers, *Fear of Uncertainty*.

In it she emphasises that an unknown future doesn't prevent a rich and abundant life, and shows how, by enjoying life's unpredictability we transform ourselves from a position of fear to one filled with excitement and potential.

"You can't change failure, but you don't have to let it define you."

EXPERIENCING FAILURE

Failure is a part of life and even the most successful people fail at some point.

I know it can feel disheartening and its human nature to want to run a thousand miles in the opposite direction and avoid failure at all costs. However, failure also makes us who we are and it can certainly help us grow into stronger individuals.

Failure gives us potential for growth. When you can bounce back from failure, anything becomes possible. I have learned that failure should totally be embraced because it helps you to understand first-hand the healing power of hope.

Holding onto hope when you have come through adversity and uncertainty to the other side, gives you the first hand evidence that anything is possible.

You will undoubtedly experience setbacks in your life but what matters is how quickly and effectively you respond to them.

BOUNCING BACK

Let me share with you, my top tips for bouncing back.

1. There is blessing in the lesson
This is one from my gorgeous friend Sharon Curran who shared them with me to always look for the blessing in the lesson. She calls them blessons. There are almost always little things that we can learn from lesson, it's about making sure that future decisions are based on the past learnings.

2. Keep a sense of humour and try and laugh at the smallest of things
LET IT GO. It is not the end of the world. Yes failure stings and yes failure can be frustrating. It can even bring us to our knees and feelings of failure and self-doubt that seem unbearable, but failure will not break you.

3. Look a failure as a way to inspire you

4. Hang on to hope and know that change will be created and focus on what matters most when failure happens
Sometimes we lose sight of everything that really matters when failure hits us hard in life. When failure happens do not let it take over your life or become your whole being, because then failure wins - instead keep your eyes focused on those things that really matter to you in life.

5. See it as potential for change, growth and new opportunities
It may seem counter-intuitive, but failure can be a useful tool when starting over. For example, failure can show many different paths to get where you want to go next. What's most important is that failure doesn't stop you from reaching your goals and dreams in life - failure may stand in your way for a short while but failure does not have the right to stop you forever.

Bounce back from failure by making it work **for** you because anything is possible after failure.

"A person who never made a mistake never tried anything new."

Albert Einstein (aka, Left-brained awesome dude)

TIME TO GO WITHIN...

LISTEN IN

COPING WITH FAILURE & UNCERTAINTY

Grab a notebook and two different colour pens. I tend to use red and green. In one colour pen write down on a daily basis everything that is negative in your life. Get it all out, written on the page, everything, all of it.

Pour your heart out; all your pain, angst, negativity, overwhelm and frustration.

Now with a different colour pen, write down all the positive things that have happened today. Sometimes this can be really difficult during challenging times so I want you to focus just on even the tiniest minute thing.

It may be that your dog snuggled up with you, your child smiled at you.
It may be that you spotted a bird in the garden.

I know for me this really helped during difficult times. It was slithers of happy moments that got me through.

When we experience negative things in life, it can be difficult to find any positivity. But by writing down both positive and negative thoughts each day, you are giving yourself an opportunity for self-reflection that may improve your outlook on what has been going wrong with your current situation or how things have changed since starting this journey.

Take time every night before bedtime where all those confusing feelings will eventually subside; give attention specifically towards positive areas and eventually you will be able to look back and see them grow.

I remember watching my girls when I was going through my divorce.

I was literally living with a head full of white noise with everything falling down around me. I would wrap them up in matching raincoats and take them splashing in muddy puddles and the look of pure joy on their faces. They were literally having the best time of their lives because they were free and carefree. Something so simple but so joyous, the simplicity of the small things and focussing on happiness switched my mood.

I made the decision to focus on the small things and be grateful every day. That has got me through some of the toughest times in my life.

When have you felt like you failed at something?
What was it?
What did you do?
How did it make you feel?

And when was the last time you splashed in a puddle? Seriously?

I am asking for a reason.

When did you last have fun?
Unapologetic fun and full-on belly laughter?

Jump in puddles. I promise, it will lift your mood.

Believe...

LIFE TOOLS

LIFE TOOLS TO HELP YOU REFRAME FAILURE AND BELIEVE IN YOURSELF

EARTH
Page 197

 MEDITATION

 MINDFULNESS

 CRYSTALS

AIR
Page 209

 JUST BREATHE

LOVE
Page 217

 MAKE TIME FOR YOU

SOUND
Page 237

 HONESTY

FIRE
Page 257

 SUNSHINE OF GRATITUDE

 IGNITING INTENTION WITH AFFIRMATIONS

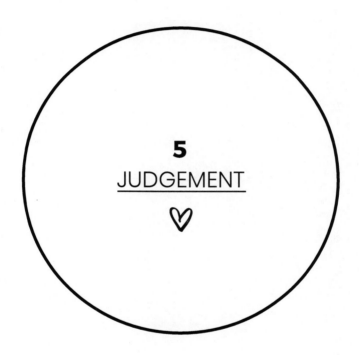

5

<u>JUDGEMENT</u>

"This is Me" by The Greatest Showman

THE LESSON

STRENGTH & SUPPORT

Thankfully my business grew from strength to strength. I was finally able to support my girls. I was with a new partner, everything on the outside seemed rosy, and we even bought a new house and watched as it was built from the ground up.

My dream life was being built right before my eyes.

Happy times, a new happy home and a new start for me and the girls. Everything was moving forward, and my dream life was becoming a reality.

Although success was happening on the outside, inside I was still crippled with self-doubt and the feelings of not being good enough. There was still something missing inside, as if I was not complete somehow.

TEARS ON TIME MANAGEMENT

I was working round the clock AGAIN. You would have thought I would have learned by now, wouldn't you? It was almost like this was my default setting. If I wasn't working, I wasn't earning. That's what I told myself.

I was struggling to balance work and life. I had lots of clients and finally financial stability, but I was working early mornings and late nights. My youngest daughter even drew a picture of me one day. I was sitting at my desk and it was an image of the back of me. Yikes.

Talk about wake up call. Something had to change.

I joined a local coaching group called Flourish run by a lovely lady called Debbie Hayes, who has since become a dear friend of mine. I found myself connected with like-minded women in business, it really started to open up areas of change in my life. I attended the time management course, and never expected what came next.

We were asked to write an employment contract to ourselves.

How many hours a week I wanted to work?
What salary I wanted to earn?
How many days holiday I wanted a year?

I reflected to my days in corporate and how much money I was earning in my twenties, I imagined myself still in corporate life now and how much salary I would be on and thought about time off and holidays.

In that moment I realised that I wasn't living the life I loved. I had been too busy working to even think about what I wanted from life.

The tears started flowing and after some unpicking of the situation with the lovely Debbie, I soon realised I was over delivering and massively unselling myself at work. I rarely took any time off and I had become a people pleaser.

From that moment forward I decided to let go of some of my workload and existing clients who felt demanding and wanted everything for nothing. I started to connect with new beautiful clients, it's like they were being sent to me and before I knew it I was surrounded by beautiful soulful women in business who I am now proud to call my friends.

They opened a whole new world to me of self-love, self-appreciation and self-worth.

It took me a while. I worked on myself daily, discovered new healing and started to create my own inner world of happiness.

JUDGE & JURY

When I was a little girl, I never really felt like I belonged. Sure, I had lots of friends, a loving family and loads to be thankful for, but for me there has always been something missing.

I have somehow felt disjointed, as though I didn't fit in, just a little different.

Some people have referred to me as 'quirky' or a misfit but whatever it is, I think I have always known I was different. I have spent many years of my life wanting to fit in. I wanted to be liked by my peers, school friends and family.

I always felt like I needed approval and a feeling of being judged by others.

I grew up with a belief that I needed to work hard to be good enough and to be accepted. You can see that in my patterns of work and pressure I put myself through previously. The long hours, the determination.

I would often chastise myself when the 'real' me kept breaking through – she is a massive rule breaker by the way.

SOCIAL MEDIA & SELF-BELIEF

The world of social media has had a huge impact on my life. It has allowed me to create growth and success in my business. I believe it is an incredible way for us to be connected, and I have built so many amazing relationships with people that I would never have the opportunity to meet otherwise.

However, social media has also created a lot of anxiety and loneliness in my life.

I have felt pretty broken at times, looking at others' so-called perfect lives and chastising myself on multiple occasions, for being a single mum and not having had the perfect home, for not creating the level of success I desire when others seem to have it all. For not feeling a sense of belonging in communities that I have wanted to be seen in.

BE
KIND
ALWAYS

WATCH YOUR WORDS

I have witnessed on many occasions people online bringing others down, often the very people who preach about kindness and then inflict pain on others and allow it to play out in a drama fuelled way. Thankfully over the years I have learned to step away from the negative energies and this allows me to heal and protect myself.

"I choose positivity."

POSITIVITY

FOCUSSING ON POSITIVITY

I can see in others clearly when they don't feel good enough. When their parents and family members judge and reinforce that feeling of not enough in them. We can allow this to define us if we hold it within.

I have learnt to release the judgement of others by doing the inner work. I have learnt that I cannot change others, I cannot change their views, I cannot change their limitations, opinions or behaviour. I can only change my own.

I can only work with myself and support my own thoughts and my own feelings.

This was a life changer for me.

I stopped blaming and started taking responsibility. It was a mighty hard lesson as it's easier to blame others and project blame and anger as a natural response, but to process anything that has been inflicted on me in a calm and loving manner has allowed my pain to become the power in my positivity and opened new possibilities.

So how do we do that?

In life, we screw up, we make mistakes, we cheat, we lie, we love, we trust, we care, we are kind, we believe, we doubt, we fault, we succeed, we dominate, we are controlled, we are praised, we are disciplined, we do good, we do wrong, we try, we fail.

Without the negative there is no positive. It's all about the highs and lows of life.

The rollercoaster. It's time to buckle up because life is quite a ride. I have spent most of my life on a rollercoaster, but quite frankly it's been more exhilarating than riding round and round on the teacups. Although I too have often wanted to get off this turbulent ride!

Enjoying the ride is one of contrasts, The exhilaration of the highs and the feelings of success and freedom coupled with feeling free, feeling loved, feeling excited, feeling peaceful, warm and cosy.

But also feeling on edge, feeling scared, feeling jumpy, feeling dark, feeling the unknown, feeling out of control, feeling hurt and damaged.

When you're a child, if you fell over and grazed your knee it feels painful. You want someone to help and make it better, but it doesn't change anything, the event still happened.

When I was seven years old, I remember having a bad accident falling off my bike. I wanted my mum to give me a hug and make it okay. I experienced a similar emotion when I lost my mum. Because I wanted protection and reassurance. I wanted my mum to pick me up and hug me and tell it was going to be alright.

But what about when that isn't possible?

We can scream and cry and lash out at others or we can choose the positive option.

Focusing on positivity is a choice.

So, I fell off my bike and I cried on the floor.
Did I dwell on it for days or did I live in the moment, embrace the change, stood up, sorted it out, wiped the tears away?

Yes I got back on that flipping bike.

Do I dwell on it now?

No, of course I don't!

The answers lie in the small stuff we experience daily and how we react to it.

I know I'm using a simple example but it's the same principles to everything in life. When it knocks you down, it's how we react and whether we can get ourselves back up.

What's the other option?

POSITIVITY IS A CHOICE

Throughout my life I have sat with a whole load of shit on my doorstep. Drowning in emotional pain. And not knowing how I can even start to see the light.

In so deep and in a dark place.

The answer was baby steps.
Daily baby steps.
Each passing moment.
Each minute.
Each hour.
Consistently and patiently.

It is only through my own self-development journey that I have realised who I really am and who I want to become. I have learned that I was never born to fit in and I was not born to conform.

The biggest lesson for me has been the understanding that not everyone is going to 'like me' and I am not in control of their thoughts and feelings anyway. So, my choice is one of self-acceptance.

However, sometimes my mind monkey creeps in.

The mind monkey, our inner critic, our own judge and jury.

I've named my mind monkey, Felicity, she's really pernickety and a massive perfectionist, and therefore questions everything I do and often tells me "it is not good enough" (she has even crept in on several occasions while I have been writing this book).

Even when I started writing this book Felicity wouldn't shut up...

- No one will want to read it
- You can't write
- People will think you're a failure
- You are not good enough
- You can't say that
- What will the girls think?
- What will your family say?
- The list goes on and on and on...

Meet Felicity, my mind monkey.
She's a pain in the arse.
(Actual Fact)

THE LEARNING

SOCIAL MEDIA & COMPARISONITIS

Social media has become a part of our everyday lives. Platforms that focus on photography and articles like Instagram and Pinterest, platforms for networking, community and groups like Facebook and LinkedIn, and platforms based around videos like YouTube and TikTok are some of the most popular social media platforms used today. SnapChat and social media stories play out our lives daily.

The way we now interact is changing relationships. Social media changes how we share experiences, express emotions, and interact with each other.

There are lots of negatives and positives around the use of social.

For example, the use of some social media content has been suggested to have an impact on increased rates of depression. However, other studies have found that people felt less alone being able to connect online.

It is all too easy to pick up your phone, to start scrolling and look at other people's so called perfect lives and feel like they have it all mapped out when ours are falling apart.

Instagram ready images portraying lives of perfection and happiness can leave you feeling low and empty inside, not good enough and can seriously affect our mood.

It is easy to seek external validation for the number of likes or comments on an image or post you have shared and to start to compare yourself to others.

Comparisonitis is an actual condition.

It's when you look at other people's lives and think that they are doing it better than you. It often just creeps up on you. You can be going about your day when you pick up your phone and an image of a friend or stranger appears and it sends you in to...

- They look younger than me.
- More beautiful than me.
- Happily married (and I'm not).
- Kids are well behaved.
- They have a healthy lifestyle.
- They have more money than me.
- They are way more successful than me.
- And all in all, can turn your mood in an instant to one of not feeling good enough.

Looking at others for inspiration is cool. But there's a difference between that and self-sabotaging our own life.

"*I will not compare myself to a stranger on social.*"

JUDGEMENT

It can be hard to process when we feel judged by others.

Often it can be other's hurt and pain that they deflect on you.

The key is to learn how to accept yourself so you can start to identify what is 'their stuff' and what is yours, so you can navigate it as peacefully as you can.

You can not control what other people think but what you can control is how you respond to it.

Instead of reacting to judgement take a little time out and see how you can respond in a loving manner instead.

Step back.

Breathe a little.

Observe don't absorb.

"Not my circus, not my monkeys."

SELF-BELIEF

Self-belief is about having the confidence in your own life and judgements. It's about valuing your own inner beauty. Being kind to yourself, respecting your own uniqueness and getting comfortable with who you are.

Self-acceptance plays a huge part here, learning to accept yourself warts and all.

So, when that negative mind chatter comes in, you are able to silence it as you no longer believe it.

When you believe in yourself anything becomes possible.

POSITIVITY IS A CHOICE

Happiness is a feeling - positivity is a choice.

Read that again.

Happiness is a feeling - positivity is a choice.

I believe that happiness is a feeling that is the outcome of certain situations or actions but it's how we feel as a circumstance, whereas positivity is a choice.

At any given moment we have options and make a choice. In a negative situation you may choose to dramatise it, to become a victim or to choose the path of positivity by working through the situation, diffusing and calming your mood and anchoring onto a more hopeful outcome.

There is no right or wrong here but there is choice in your life path.

Positivity is about being optimistic in mind and attitude. Often people refer to this as being a glass half full kind or person, instead of glass half empty?

Which are you?

I personally believe a glass is refillable. It hasn't always been that way. It has taken many hours of inner work to get here but I now always choose the positive side of life.

There is one thing that can stop your positivity in its tracks.

THE MIND MONKEY

Remember Felicity?
(Yup, she's still a pain in the arse!)

Just in case you haven't connected with your mind monkey yet... let me explain. Your mind monkey is your inner critic, whose job it seems to be that little voice inside your head or sitting on your shoulder to tell you...

You're not good enough, smart enough, creative enough, loveable enough...

Negative self-talk that has been internalised – thoughts that you may have about yourself that aren't necessarily true but you believe them to be. Most of this negative self-talk comes from messages received throughout childhood through society or parental guidance.

Once negative self-talk has been internalised, it becomes the inner critic which you hear in your head when you're doing something challenging.

YOUR MIND IS IN CONTROL

Does your mind control you, or do you control your mind?

The truth is that if you want to have a healthier, positive and better mindset, then it's up to you to take control of your own mind.

You have the ability to understand and use the power of thought in a productive way, or a counterproductive way, whatever you decide, it's entirely up to you. The factors that influence your moods and behaviours aren't some distant entities outside of yourself; they're based on what goes on inside your head. It is this internal system that largely determines how successful (or unsuccessful) you are at creating the kind of life that makes you happy.

Now I'm not a psychologist or an expert in this field but I have and continue to work on my own mindset on a daily basis.

I refer to it as mindset reframing, which to me is a way of using your imagination to see a situation from a different perspective and in a new light.

The idea of reframing comes from Cognitive Behavioural Therapy (CBT), where people are encouraged to change their negative thought processes into more positive ones. CBT is mainly used to treat mental illness such as anxiety, depression and phobias.

The concept behind this kind of therapy is that unhelpful thought patterns can lead to psychological problems and mental health issues, so changing these thoughts can alleviate symptoms and help the patient get better. Negative thought patterns prevent people from seeing things objectively: by thinking in a different way, they might be able to solve or work around the problem instead of obsessing over it unproductively.

AFFIRMATIONS

Affirmations or self-talk positively influences your mindset, which in turn improves your performance and growth. It has been scientifically proven that when people say positive things to themselves, they become motivated and more committed to achieving their goals.

The power of affirmations is unlimited. You can develop them in your life in whichever way you want. You can use affirmations to anchor into your own mind to become the best version of yourself by repeating your thoughts over and over again until they become a part of the reality of who you are.

You can reach out and grab anything that your heart desires through self-belief. All it takes on your part is being able to believe in yourself enough, so maybe one day if someone asks what keeps you motivated throughout the day, you can say... Nothing. There is nothing at all that keeps me motivated, other than my own mind.

I am loveable

I am enough

I am

creative

I am smart

THE POWER OF POSSIBILITY

Yes, external stuff happens in our life but we are the creator of how to react and respond. We can stand in our own way or fling open the gates of possibility and expand our journey. If we can understand the barriers and work to break them down this is how we can move forward to embrace our full potential and live out a life we love.

There is a whole spectrum of 'blocks'.

Self-sabotage
Where we deliberately go out of our way (consciously or subconsciously) to stop something from happening.

Imposter Syndrome
Stopping ourselves from growing – keeping ourselves small, feeling not good enough, there's no point.

It takes a whole huge heap of badassery to step up to speak out and become the very person we truly want to be.

I am a badass

LISTEN IN

YOUR MIND MONKEY

Have a think about your inner critic and what they are saying to you right now?
How noisy are they?
What are they telling you?
Is there any pattern to messages they have on repeat?

Now I want you to listen to his or her tone. How do they speak? Are they loud or quiet? Are they big or small? Start to think about what they actually look like and give them a name.

In your notebook, journal or below, write down some of the negative self-talk your mind tells you.

What does your mind monkey look like?

My mind monkey is called...

Now it's time to silence them. When they creep up in your head, recognise them, acknowledge them, then tell them to "shut the fuck up." They are not in control, they are not steering the ship, and they are just a passenger. You are the captain of your vessel – you decide.

love life...

LIFE TOOLS

LIFE TOOLS TO HELP YOU OVERCOME JUDGEMENT AND LOVE YOUR LIFE

EARTH
Page 197

 MEDITATION

SOUND
Page 237

 YOUR VOICE

 AMPLIFY YOUR THOUGHTS

FIRE
Page 257

IGNITING INTENTION WITH AFFIRMATIONS

 THE HAND OF POSSIBILITY

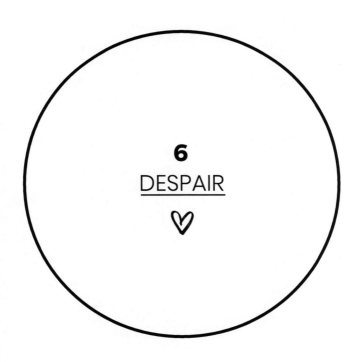

6

<u>DESPAIR</u>

"Wings" by Birdy

HOPE

THE LESSON

THE HOPE OF HAPPINESS

During the dark days of my life it was hard to see the light. I often felt stuck, stagnant and frozen, incapable of seeing my future. I would just look up at the trees, the birds, the sky, witness everything constantly still moving,

Over time I realised I didn't need to see the future, I just needed to believe that everything would work out, somehow.

I had to let go, I had to live in the present moment and surrender. I had to stop trying to control and just trust.

Trusting has really helped me on my journey. Trusting that change is possible. Trusting that there is hope, even in the darkest of times, even when it has just a tiny glimmer within, even when it has felt non-existent. I have trusted that it is possible, I have watched the sun go down and arise again every morning,

I have studied the moon move through phases, diminish and become whole again and I have repeated to myself over and over again that...

"This too shall pass."

This belief and holding onto hope has got me through the darkest of times.

I believe everything passes. Life ebbs and flows, good and bad. I have felt joy having fun with family, celebrating birthdays, marrying my husband, giving birth to my beautiful daughters, getting my degree, but these moments have passed and become memories; life has moved on and so does pain.

Pain subsides and balance and calm is restored. Although life may look different on the other side, the waves can still be calmed and beauty and happiness can be felt once more.

HOPELESSNESS

In 2016 I lost my younger brother Nick, to suicide. The pain was intense; the anger overwhelming, utter devastation. My world was blown apart.

How could my thirty-one year old beautiful funny, vibrant, handsome, intelligent, creative, loving brother feel that he could not go on?

The devastation hit, but so did the anger.

I had so many unanswered questions.

I used to scream out loud, "How could you do this, how could you do this to me?"

Then the deep sense of sadness would ensue, and I would find myself in the pit of despair. How could I not save him? Why could he not talk to me? Why did I not see this?

I used to have a belief that suicide was selfish. I now don't believe it's selfish.

I know he loved me beyond measure and would never have wanted to inflict any pain on others.

It was hard for me to understand and come to terms with the fact that he couldn't see the glimmer of light within.

What I do know is I can't change it, I wish with all my heart I could.

Within weeks of losing my brother, my relationship with my partner I had been with for six years, broke down suddenly and I found myself moving out of my dream home. I was back to sofa surfing with my girls until our new rented accommodation was ready to move into.

When we finally got the keys to our new home, it was like we had landed in our own little sanctuary; a beautiful place where we could be at peace and start to rebuild our shattered lives.

Thankfully I worked with an incredible counsellor, Liz Foley, she specialised in complex grief (the type of grief where you are given no answers). She was able to help me silence my inner torment and support me to transform it into inner calm. It took time but I found a way to live with the acceptance of the pain and to start to transform it into an inner peace.

We can't change what caused the pain, but we can change how we choose to react to it. I wanted to change my life. I wanted to change it for others too.

I vowed that if I could save one person's life and one family from feeling the pain that no family should ever endure, then that was what I was here to do. This is the very reason that I became a suicide intervention first aider. I made choices to move from the pain into positivity and it became part of my healing.

IT'S OK NOT TO BE OK

One of my biggest bugbears is when people who experience others that have endured or are currently in pain are troubled, weary, depressed, struggling, or doubting and they expect them just to be ok, to silence the suffering.

THIS IS TOXIC POSITIVITY.

They may use phrases like, "man up" or "get a grip" or "you so much to be grateful for" or "there are people a lot worse off than you" or "sort yourself out" and "stop feeling sorry for yourself".

Let's face it as human beings...

We all have shit days.
We all have shit weeks.
We all have shit months.
We all experience periods of time when we are not ok.

Yes the scale of severity can differ. It is really more than ok not to be ok.

But what isn't ok is...
To judge others or worse, bring them down.
To not offer kindness or if you can't offer kindness don't make judgement.
And if you are suffering – to not reach out, to not to get help and support when you need it.

This support can help you move forward, to believe there is hope – it can be a lifeline. I want you to believe in hope.

Hope is what gives us an anchor, it helps drive us forward. Hope and possibility get you out of the shit place we are in and is the foundation to start believing there are brighter times ahead and that change is totally possible. One small step after another, this can take you anywhere.

I have been in the pit of despair more times that I want to remember but I've always had hope. I've always reached out and got help when I have needed it.

A few days after my brother died, I found myself on the phone to The Samaritans. I was surrounded by my family and friends, but I still felt desperate and alone. I was not able to unravel my own thoughts.

In that moment they turned my thoughts around, they helped me to see what a blessing it was to have had the honour of having him in my life for the thirty one years that I did.

There have been many moments when I have felt afraid, when I have felt desperate and alone. I have always sought help. This has come in many forms from counselors, reiki healers, conversations with friends and family, tarot readings, spirit guides, witches goddesses, crystal healing. I did it all, but my point is...

Life is not black-and-white. We experience a whole range of experiences and emotions in our lifetime. There is a whole spectrum of shades that we can work through, and the key to surviving this is actually moving from one to the other, even if it's only slight, to move from the darkness to the light.

To see the magic in rainbows, to believe in dreams, to look up at the stars and trust that this pain too shall pass, by holding on to hope and possibility.

HOPE
&
POSSIBILITY

Rainbows...

MY POCKET FULL OF RAINBOWS

I now always look for the glimmers of hope and possibility. I have a whole array of tools I have learned and carry with me at all times (I have shared them with you in the next section)

If someone told me eight years ago, I would meditate and spend two hours a day on self-development, stand in the mirror and recite affirmations to myself, practice crystal healing, walk round with crystals in my bra and journal, I would've have laughed, but I have transformed myself by working on my own inner forgiveness and self-belief.

When you forgive yourself, you heal and when you let go you grow. Journaling has been an amazing help for me. It has allowed me to unpeel the layers and release my feelings so I can really understand the real me. It has allowed me to dream and connect with my desires and to help bring them into reality.

Just after Nick's funeral I had to return to work. I was still broken and as I sat there contemplating how I could actually go live and run an online class, I thought about what Nick would say...

Nay you can do this.
You are
Naomi 'fucking' Gilmour

And there it was the reassurance that I could – I wrote it on a post it note and stuck it on my computer screen.

This was my affirmation, my anchor that I could get through the day and I did.

A few days later I had some clients in my little garden office. It wasn't until they left that I realised the post it note was still there. Still makes me chuckle to this day.

Nick is still my guiding light and forever Batman.

My Hopeful Heart ♡

THE LEARNING

HOLDING ON TO HOPE

Some people define hope as being optimistic. While this may be true, it is crucial to remember that hope and optimism are not interchangeable terms.

Optimism implies that something good will happen, while hope assumes nothing about the future or outcome of actions. Hope for me is about holding on, about trusting that the situation will pass and opening up possibilities. I like to define HOPE as...

Hold
On
Pain
Ends.

Or to think about it being the gateway to possibility.

Hand
On heart....
Possible
Ever after.

By holding on to hope and your heart, you take control through allowing yourself to trust, you allow yourself to surrender to the situation, you allow uncertainty, and you allow yourself to learn to get comfortable with that place.

This is a place unique to you, it is an inner strength that only you can find. It may be a tiny flicker; it may be a nudge or a feeling. You have a choice to grasp onto that however small and anchor into HOPE.

HOPE still feels uncertain as the outcome may not be evident, but when you can get comfortable with this and accept uncertainty is ok, it will open up possibilities.

It keeps you in a place of multiple outcomes and helps to move you towards choice.

POSSIBILITY

Possibility is really like an opening of potential options, it gives you a place to anchor onto a 'next step', a future, a potential outcome.

It gives us ideas of different paths or options so we can start to take some sort of control to help you move forwards.

Possibility allows your thought process to move to another state.

You don't have to be in a desperate state to step into hope and possibility, it is an integral part of our growth.

We can even visualise our dream future (HOPE) and creating goals towards them (POSSIBILITY) and then set goals to take the action to get there (POSITIVITY – THE CHOICE).

LISTEN IN

THE HAND OF HOPE

Your hands have been with you for a lifetime. They have done some incredible things. When you were a baby you crawled on your hands and knees, you learnt to feed yourself, you have cooked, you have created things, learnt to write, all with your hands, they have grown with you and you have connected to others, you have held others hands, you have wiped away tears, you have held them tightly.

Take a look at your hands. Study them closely, look at every detail. Think about how incredible they are.

AND SO ARE YOU

Whenever you are experiencing a moment of darkness, look at your hands, anchor into hope and know that you are safe, it is just a moment that will pass, even write yourself a note on your hand to remind you.

The hand of hope opens up options so you can trust in the moment. When you are in uncertain times it's key to anchor into the unknown but trust that you are going to be ok.

Affirmations can be a great way to hold onto hope and trust in possibility in uncertain moments. Here's some I have used, feel free to use these or create your own.

I am safe. I am enough. I am loved. I expect a miracle. I've got this. I am safe. I am strong. Just breathe. Hold on. It's going to be ok. I am ok. I am worthy. I can do this

Write them on a post it note. Stick them on your mirror. Write it on your hand. Wear it!

I am
loved

I've got this

Hold on

I am worthy

I am
enough

I am safe

Just breathe

I am strong

I can do this

SPACE TO DRAW YOUR OWN HAND OF HOPE

the light...

LIFE TOOLS

LIFE TOOLS TO HELP NAVIGATE THE DARKNESS AND FIND THE LIGHT

EARTH
Page 197

 GROUNDING

 MEDITATION

 CRYSTALS

LOVE
Page 217

 SELF CARE RITUALS

FIRE
Page 257

 SELF DISCOVERY

 IGNITING INTENTION WITH AFFIRMATIONS

7

VULNERABILITY

"Broken & Beautiful" by Kelly Clarkson

THE LESSON

SEARCHING FOR LOVE

Surprisingly, this is possibly one of the hardest sections for me to write in this book. Why? Because it makes me feel uncomfortably vulnerable.

But I'm sharing it because I know it will help you identify with your own vulnerability. I also know it takes massive courage to show your vulnerability and courageous is what I am here to be.

All my life I have searched for love.

One of my earliest memories (aged three or four) was blaming myself for my parents' divorce. It gave me a sense of not belonging.

My mum raised four of us on her own from the ages of three, five, seven and nine. When I look back now as a mother myself I think how the hell did she actually do that? My Mum was amazing. We didn't have much. She juggled work and family life and she gave us all she had. We were all really close as a family and shared lots of love, we had a busy but happy home. Mum juggled jobs and caring for us and one day she found new love.

Mum's new partner arrived in my life like a giant cuddly teddy bear – he rocked up in his little black sports car and I was like, WOW! I thought he was amazing. He showed a massive interest in my life. I loved spending time with him, and we had so much fun together, days out trips overseas and family parties.

They married when I was seven years old. It felt like he had somehow made my life complete. He used to work overseas so was away for months on end, I really missed him when he was away. I have happy memories of meeting him from the airport on his return. I was always so excited to see him and he would always bring me presents from his travels and had bags of time to spend with me when he was home.

He taught me to cook, he showed me what it was like to have a father figure within the family home. He created fun adventures and although I always had a loving family, for the first time ever I felt a real sense of belonging.

THE DRAMA QUEEN

We had seven happy years, then things started to go wrong. They separated when I was fifteen years old. I struggled to come to terms with their separation, it was like a dark void inside of me.

I felt like I couldn't open up and talk to my mum as I didn't want to upset her, so I kept silent. I held it all within.

I felt lonely. It triggered my earlier childhood and sense of not belonging. I used to feel like I 'needed' a boyfriend that would want to be with me so I would feel a sense of acceptance and love. I felt unhappy and had a desperate need for security.

This feeling carried with me throughout my life, I became a 'needy' drama queen. I grew into my twenties, always making it someone else's responsibility to make me happy. This resulted in bad choices, projecting my own hurt and pain onto boyfriends, expecting them to fix the emptiness I felt inside. Thankfully since then I have 'done the work'. I have stripped away the layers of this stuff to learn and understand why I feel this way.

Until recently I have always wondered why I felt I couldn't have one of my biggest desires. To feel love and be loved in a partnership. Even though I have had happy relationships I have always felt like there was something missing. All I ever wanted was to find and settle with my soul mate, my buddy, my one.

I have looked at friends on Facebook (there's that comparisonitis again).

I have seen others appear to have what I want which has made me feel like I did something wrong, that I was somehow not deserving of love, that I was not good enough to be loved, that I was not attractive enough, slim enough, beautiful enough, kind enough.

Maybe if I did more, said more, had more money, was more successful, was smarter or funnier.

Even when I have been in a relationship, I have not really felt loved, there has been a feeling that deep down they don't really care (and at any moment I will get rejected) all of this has made me feel shit inside, an empty hollow feeling of being unsafe and unhappy.

Over the years I have criticised myself, I have torn myself apart and judged myself, I have felt terrified that if I speak up and say how I actually feel that I will appear 'needy' or I may be abandoned again, that they won't understand. I have created a whole world of silence that I have internally navigated so that I don't get judged for how I feel with a crippling feeling that once it's been said it's too late and it won't change anything anyway.

So I have silenced myself.

SILENCED BY SHAME

Shame has also silenced me. It is something I have experienced right the way through my life, from a young age when I was told that "I should be ashamed of myself". I was. In my younger years I was, for making bad life choices, for going 'off the rails' for not getting the grades in my education and later in life when I lost my business, the feelings of shame that I have internalised were crippling. Guilt has silently eaten away at my own 'self-rejection' and affirmed my feeling of not being good enough.

For making some terrible life choices. For upsetting others. For walking away from relationships and hurting others. For not being able to sustain the family unit for my girls. For not being able to say the right thing that could have saved my brother the night he died.

Holding onto the inner blame and allowing it has consumed me at times and negatively impacted my self-worth.

This anchored in a feeling within that ultimately, I was not worthy of this connection – the connection of love and belonging.

LIFE IS SHORT

I want to live my life to the fullest.

For years and years I have battled with lack of self-worth, the inability to love myself and lack of togetherness in a relationship.

I want true love but I don't need saving.

I have spent years and years having to be everything. Mum, cleaner, teacher, therapist, friend, coach, provider, doer, dog sitter, dog walker, cat feeder, cook...

I am more than capable of looking after myself and I can provide financially for me and the girls but it doesn't mean I want to be on my own. I can't tell you how many times people have told me that. I am "better on my own".

Whilst I am more than happy to go on dates with myself, I want to share my life with an amazing 'partner' who in a balanced, harmonious, without sacrifice kind of way. I feel like I am complete on my own like a cupcake, but a little cherry and decoration on the top to enhance my life would be truly beautiful.

I have always believed in fairy tales and I do believe in magic and miracles.

And 'I know' someday somewhere (no don't worry I'm not going to start singing Julie Andrews) it will be my time to meet my 'one'.

MY EQUAL WHO I CAN CHERISH AND BE CHERISHED, LOVE AND LOVED, VALUE AND VALUED, RESPECT AND RESPECTED.

THE LEARNING

CUT WIDE OPEN

Betrayal and rejection can come in many forms through life. The pain is the same but can also vary in levels of severity.

Whether it's a friend who has spoken about you behind your back, a partner who has racked up debts and not paid the bills, a colleague that has undermined you, not being invited out on social events by your usual circle of friends or being ditched by your lover, it's all betrayal and can make you feel rejected.

REJECTION

If you have ever felt 'rejected' you will know it can feel like someone has trampled over your heart.

If you have ever seen the film *Maleficent*, the scene where he cuts her wings off. She awakes crippled with the devastation that her 'one', her prince could take her wings and her freedom away from her.

This is betrayal and rejection.

Rejection causes a searing pain and heaviness in your heart almost like you can't breathe, it can leave you confused, questioning, analysing your mind racing with all of the angst of the moment.

When you experience rejection, it stirs up feelings of loss and helplessness. It can have a huge physical impact, making your stomach wrench like you want to be sick, feeling like you've been stabbed, a feeling of total disbelief, a sadness, a darkness.

The devastating blow of rejection can stir up a head full of fuzz (white noise). Remember the grief cycle I talked about in part one? This is the same. Rejection is loss. It feels and acts the same.

SPEAKING YOUR TRUTH

Silence creates disempowerment. Not speaking your truth keeps you stuck. Now there is a HUGE difference between speaking your truth and just speaking up to lash out and project your pain on someone (I've done that in the past too).

Speaking your truth is about connecting with your needs, wants and beliefs and being able to express them in a calm loving manner.

Lashing out is projecting your own words, hurt and pain on another. Learning to understand the difference has been life changing for me, but it only comes when you are prepared to take time and start to fully understand yourself and others.

Speaking your truth becomes much easier when you have learned to accept yourself, when you have found a way to heal your own inner shame and guilt and get comfortable with being vulnerable.

TRUTH

SHAME & VULNERABILITY

Have you ever felt shame? Of course, you have, we all do. Shame feels uncomfortable. It's all the stuff we would rather hide about ourselves like some kind of inner secret we try our best to hold within ourselves for fear of being found out.

Shame keeps us small, shame allows the inner critic to explode in our minds, to remind us of everything we are not. The mind monkey that tells us we are not good enough, or questions who are we to do this?

Acknowledging our own shame and being vulnerable is NOT a weakness, it allows us to fully embrace who we are.

If you haven't discovered Brené Browne yet then I strongly recommend you check her out. She describes vulnerability as uncertainty, risk and emotional exposure. She uses vulnerability to measure courage.

I trust my journey and myself so much these days that I actually believe situations are put in my path to redirect me. I believe all the curve balls have shaped me and made me stronger and more resilient to become the person I am today.

LOVE & BELONGING (SELF-WORTH)

In life we crave connection. Connection comes in many forms throughout our life. When we feel connected, it gives us a sense of belonging. It enables us to feel loved, to feel safe and secure. But In order to enable connection we need to feel worthy of it.

Worthiness
Self-worth is the internal sense of being good enough and worthy of love and belonging from others.

Self-worth is often confused with self-esteem, which relies on external factors such as successes and achievements to define worth and can often be inconsistent leading to someone struggling with feeling worthy.

Self-acceptance
Self-acceptance is when we learn to love every part of ourselves. Both positive and negatives, the positives are relatively easy to accept but the negatives tend to take work.

It is about taking a look at yourself, peeling back the emotional layers and fully embracing and loving who you are, warts and all.

It is ok to be yourself, to be totally all of you... light and dark and to love the shadows within yourself.

When you learn self-acceptance it helps you to be less self critical, so you can love yourself more. It helps build your self confidence so you are more likely to take action and work through any fears, it builds self compassion so you can build resilience during setbacks in your life and it helps enable yourself to feel worthy.

LEARNING SELF-ACCEPTANCE SUPPORTS YOU TO

FEEL WORTHY and know that you are enough.

FLOWER POWER

In Rebecca Cambell's Starseed Oracle Deck, there is a card called the Courageous Peony in which she describes a flower who embraces all of who they are.

One of my favourite flowers is the tulip. Because it grows to the sunlight it creates its own free will and grows toward the light.

While I was writing this book I had a vase of peonies on my coffee table, I watched them daily as they started to open up and then closed by night before exploding into full glory. Bared open for all their inner beauty to be seen.

We are the same, if we decide to keep closed up in a tiny bud we will only ever be seen that way. Time to break open and expose our beautiful light within.

"A flower doesn't compete with the flower next to it. It just blooms."

LISTEN IN

YOU ARE A COURAGEOUS FLOWER

Imagine you are a flower.

What do you look like in full bloom?

How does expressing your vulnerability feel?

What would be possible if you could illuminate your inner beauty?

courage...

LIFE TOOLS

LIFE TOOLS TO EMBRACE COURAGE

WATER
Page 197

 SELF DISCOVERY

SOUND
Page 237

 AMPLIFY YOUR THOUGHTS

 MUSIC AND MOVEMENT

 THE HAND OF POSSIBILITY

SPACE
Page 245

 YOUR HIGHER SELF

 MOON AND STARS

 ENERGY HEALING

FIRE
Page 257

 IGNITING INTENTION WITH AFFIRMATIONS

 LIGHTING UP YOUR LIFE

PART 2

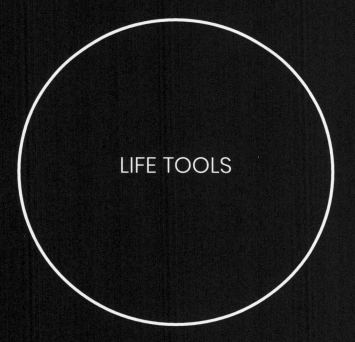

LIFE TOOLS

"Cover Me in Sunshine" by Pink

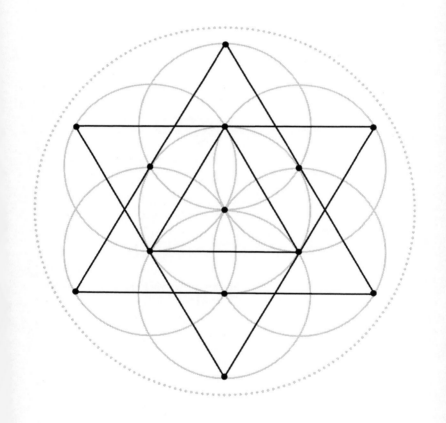

A few years ago I learned to read tarot cards and I have a real love for angel and oracle cards. In tarot there is a card called the tower, many fear it, as it appears that literally the world is crumbling, the foundation falling away.

I've read this card for myself so many times, and like others I used to dread it. Over time I have realised these moments of crumbling and devastation have actually given me the foundations for new life, new beginnings and new opportunities.

Yes, it can be painful to experience what feels like a downfall, but when you move through to the other side everything feels more beautiful and you can appreciate your journey and become more grateful.

Broken open is never going to feel comfortable but it's an opportunity for you to do the work on yourself, for you to understand who you are and do the healing that is required so that you can live the best version of your life.

Sometimes you have to work through the layers of hurt and pain to enable you to reveal the truth of who you really are. It's so worth it to see the real beauty at the very core of yourself.

Bearing all is never going to be easy, it's never going to feel ok, being vulnerable is not generally a comfortable place to be but thankfully I am finally able to do this, it takes layers of work and is always ongoing.

Ditching the judgement of others, accepting the shadows and learning to be totally ok with being imperfectly perfect.

Trusting others and allowing your heart to be open so that you can allow intimacy. Not holding back and not living in fear.

Stepping out into who I am. All of me 'unapologetically' and being able to...

"Love like I have never been hurt."

Over the years I have often shared a muted version of myself, I have rocked up to work and social events 'larger than life' externally and worn an invisible mask from what I was actually feeling inside.

There is something truly special when you allow the mask to drop away and fully learn to accept yourself. As you are.

I've messed up.
I've not like myself.
I've criticised my actions.
I've hurt myself and others.
I've accepted relationships that didn't feel good enough.
I've sacrificed my own happiness at times.
I've screamed and cried.
I've been selfish.
I've been a people pleaser.
I've regretted many times.

I have since embarked on my journey of self-discovery and realised...

I wanted to learn how to fully accept myself and be me.
I wanted to allow myself to show my vulnerability and I want to feel connection.
I wanted to feel true love and passion and I wanted to share true love and passion with others.
I wanted to listen, and I wanted to be heard.
I wanted to dance in the music of life together in balance with others.
I wanted this and I now know I deserve all of this.

I realised I no longer needed to hold back.

I had nothing to prove to anyone but me.

I have discovered many tools that have supported my transformation, that have supported me and allowed me to heal. They have helped me to become the person I am today.

I wanted to share them with you so that whatever you are experiencing in your life, you can develop your own tool kit of self-discovery too.

LIFE ELEMENTS

Bringing all of life's elements into your life can truly help you navigate the storms and establish inner peace. They can make your world feel magical. Each element has its own energy, when you are practicing these tools think about the elements that they come under.

Think about the physical things you can connect to them, it may be candles, meditation, music, incense, nature, the flow of the sea or the stillness of the sky.

EARTH

The element of Earth is usually referred to as grounding and calming. It is connected to our safety and stability. It is the material essence of the world.

AIR

The element of Air acts as a channel for clear communication and self-expression. It's responsible for your breath and movement. It influences the ability to act with love and compassion.

LOVE

The element of Love opens our heart and allows us forgiveness, it enables us to heal it radiates compassion and kindness and gives us unconditional acceptance and peace.

WATER

Water is characterised by its ability to flow and adapt as well as its healing nature that nourishes the body. Connection, desires, feelings and flow. It is connected to the emotions and relies on your intuition. It lives in the realms of dreams. Water is insightful and healing. It embodies the depth of emotions and intuition.

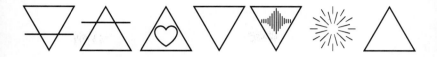

SOUND

The element of Sound transmits vibration and creates a vibe. Sound is connected to our communication, creativity listening, and the ability to be heard and share ideas.

SPACE

Spirituality involves the recognition of a feeling or sense or belief that there is something greater than me, something more to being human than a sensory experience, and that the greater whole of which we are part is cosmic or divine in nature.

FIRE

The Fire element acts as a cleanser that burns up toxins and impurities. It is the source of heat and power and brings confidence and courage. Fire is connected to passionate energy. It can spark new ideas and allows rebirth.

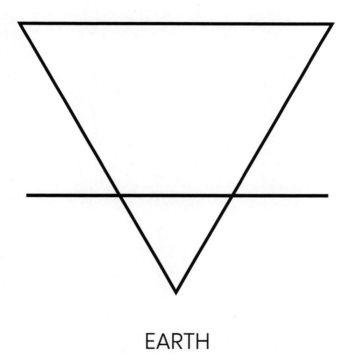

EARTH

create calm

How safe do you feel? How could you feel more nourished? Earth energy gives us the security of peaceful surroundings. The basics of life like vitality and strength are received from nutritious food, or the joy found in laughter with friends.

Are you harnessing the power of the earth?

 **GROUNDING**

Grounding basically means to bring your focus to what is happening to you physically, either in your body or in your surroundings, instead of being trapped by the thoughts in your mind that are causing you to feel anxious. It helps you stay in the present moment instead of worrying about things that may happen in the future or events that have already happened, but you still find yourself going over and over them in your head.

Grounding, also known as Earthing, is a way to reconnect you to the Earth, recalibrating your energy to connect with the energy of the Earth and its electrical field. Grounding and Earthing helps you to discharge built-up energy, negativity, release toxins and balance and centre yourself.

Grounding techniques are coping strategies to help bring you back into the present moment, back into your body and cope with distress from your emotional state or any situation. Grounding can help with confusion, irritation, overwhelm, anxiety, PTSD and trauma triggers, dissociation, feeling "spaced out" or scattered, lack of clarity and focus.

Grounding brings you into the present moment, calming the nervous system. Allowing for the state of Gratitude. Gratitude for this moment. Gratitude for relief. For Breath. For life.

Being in a state of gratitude allows you to be open to receiving from the Universe and is a powerful state for manifesting.

There are different ways to ground yourself when you feel anxious and overwhelmed here are a few of my favourites...

 NURTURING NATURE

Spending time in nature is a perfect way to distract yourself and focus on the beauty around you. If you can walk near trees or water it can also help you to breathe and experience a sense of calmness.

If you can, take your shoes off and stand on grass to really feel the earth below you. Think about how solid the ground is and how it is protecting you at this moment. If you can see a tree hold your hand on it to feel it's solid grounded energy, you can even give it a hug if you feel you want to.

MINDFULNESS

We all lead busy lives rushing around on auto pilot, charging from place to place, multi-tasking at work, taking care of our families and trying to stay in touch with friends.

But taking a time to pause and be mindful can dramatically improve our well-being, making us feel calmer, less stressed and more at peace with your emotions.

We can practice mindfulness at any given moment. It is available to all of us and in any moment, you can take the time to appreciate it. When you practice mindfulness, you are practicing the art of creating space for yourself.

Being mindful is about just paying attention to the present moment and clearing your mind from distractions. Most activities can be done mindfully, even eating a sweet or walking down the street or simply sitting still and focusing on your breath or looking at an object, studying it in detail. Activities can also be mindful, knitting, sewing and colouring are all mindful activities.

Adult colouring is super popular these days. You can pick up colouring in books from most high street stores and there are mindful colouring resources on my website too.

You can even doodle away through the pages of this book, that's why there are so many black and white images for you to explore including the one to the right here too.

MEDITATION

Meditation can be used for reducing stress, manifesting your desires, healing, coping with loss and is also incredible for grounding. You can follow a guided meditation. You can follow a guided meditation for grounding, see the resources section on my website or you can simply relax and experience the stillness in silence.

If you haven't meditated before it can sometimes feel a little strange, the more you practice grounded meditation, the more natural it becomes.

MEDITATION FOR GROUNDING

- Close your eyes and focus on your breathing.

- Breathe in through your nose, slowly and deeply. Exhale and feel your stomach relax.

- Focus on breathing this way for a couple of minutes until it becomes rhythmic and effortless.

- Notice if you have fallen into any distractions and return your awareness to your breathing.

- Visualize yourself sitting on a tree trunk.

- Focus on the energy in your body flowing downward to the earth. The tree has become an extension of your body, extending through your feet.

- Continue to imagine this tree trunk traveling down through Earth, until your trunk finally reaches the centre of the Earth.

- While you are breathing, let any negative feelings escape your body. Leave any feelings of pain, frustration, anger or bitterness in the centre of the Earth.

- Push your energy upward. Imagine Earth's energy flowing back up through your trunk.

- Before opening your eyes, rest in the feelings of centeredness and calm for a few moments.

- When you feel ready, bring your mind back to your body and open your eyes.

- Any time you feel unfocused, close your eyes and visualize the connection that you have shared with Earth.

CRYSTALS

I absolutely adore the energy of crystals. Crystals are amazing little batteries full of energy that you can access easily to support you in daily life. place them around your home or get them small enough to pop in your pocket, or even your bra! You can also get crystal jewellery, each with their own unique gifts. Here are some crystals that can help you to ground and support you.

Black Tourmaline
Tourmaline crystal is a beautiful black stone which can help create a shield around a person or room to prevent negative and unwanted energies entering it.   Tourmaline also helps grounding and supports the balancing of chakras. This beautiful stone can dissolve challenging energies and help transform negative thinking.

Bloodstone
Bloodstone gives stamina and powerful strength during periods of endless difficulty when you feel that you cannot go on. These stone clears self-doubt and helps you to persevere through your issues until you are through the worst. Bloodstone can also clear blockages from past life experiences.

Garnet
Garnet reflects a powerful red ray energy. These gems help build up life-force energy, helping you to see your purpose in life and providing you with the courage to deal with life's ups and downs. As Garnet is connected to the Root Chakra this gemstone will give you the feeling of having firm foundations and being grounded.

Garnet is a powerfully energizing stone that protects and is said to warn of approaching danger but draws harm to enemies. Traditionally Garnet was used in engagement rings as Garnet inspires love and devotion and removes inhibitions and taboos.

Moss Agate

In ancient times Moss Agate was used as a gardener's good luck charm. This stone is said to refresh the soul, renew your connection with nature and enable you to see the beauty in your surroundings. When used as a touchstone it helps to create an immediate bond with Mother Earth. A birthing crystal, this is an excellent choice for expectant mothers and midwives, as this helps to lessen pain and ensure a good delivery.

Moss agate helps people access their intuitive feelings and channelling their energy correctly.

This is a powerfully protective stone especially during a relationship break up.

Obsidian

Obsidian is a strongly protective stone, Black Obsidian forms a shield against negativity. It absorbs negative energies from the environment and provides deep soul healing. Black Obsidian works extremely fast and with great power to locate the cause of disease and removes disorders from the body.

Tiger's Eye

Tigers Eye crystal is known for having a powerful vibration and draws spiritual energies to the Earth and is thought to hold the sun within. It can help in daily life with blocked creativity and low self-esteem.

Smoky Quartz

Smoky quartz is brown in colour. It is linked to the earth's energy and is good for grounding and protection. It can help us to focus on life when it is feeling dark and can support a sense of confidence and emotional security. Smoky Quartz is one of the best cleansing stones. It is a good antidote to stress and can help alleviate suicidal tendencies. Smoky quartz supports strength and is a healing crystal for radiation related illnesses for anyone going through chemo or radiotherapy.

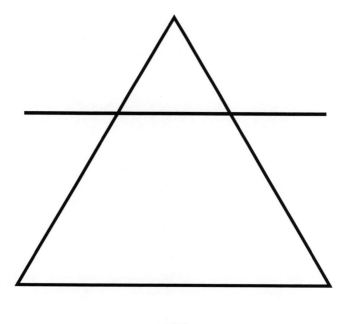

AIR

let it go...

Have a think about air. How does it make you feel?

Imagine yourself soaring through the sky on a bird's wings – looking at your life from a higher perspective. What do you see? Are there possibilities for change and growth? Can you create more happiness, more freedom? More peace?

The world is wide open and waiting for you today.

When you can start to believe in yourself and what is possible, this creates a foundation for your future. Letting go of what no longer serves you so you can invite in the new is a life changer.

It's time to...

 **JUST BREATHE**

S – Stop what you are doing right now

T – Take a BREATH just know right at this very moment you have got this. INHALE and EXHALE what a powerful force air is

O – Observe your thoughts, feelings, and emotions. Feel the breath, tune in to your lungs expanding and contracting.

P – Proceed with something that will support you in the moment. Listening to your breath and know you have everything within you to create your best life.

Breath is such a powerful force it's what powers our lungs and is our lifeline. If you would like to learn more about breath work you can check out my lovely guide The Ice Warrior and explore the Wim Hof technique.

LET IT GO

What's on your mind?

What's bothering you?

Write yourself a list, write it in a letter to someone who has wronged or upset you.

Attach it to a balloon, write it on the balloon or if you don't have a balloon use the balloon template in the resources area.

Close your eyes – let all of these feelings, upset, hurt, pain angst go.

Attach it to the balloon and watch it float away... or if it's on paper take it out in the garden and burn it.

However, you choose to 'LET IT GO.'

 **YOUR BUBBLE**

Have you ever felt unsettled or stressed out for no apparent reason? This may be due to who you are spending time with, and who is around you. As we go about our day, we come in contact with lots of energies and emotions. We can take on these energies as our own.

Can you remember any experiences you can recall where your mood drastically changed for the worse?

Think about who was around you at the time? It is likely you picked up negativity of another.

They don't belong to us and there's a beautiful way we can create your own protective shield.

What you allow into your world is crucial for your inner peace and happiness.

Close your eyes and imagine you are stepping into a bubble made just the right size for you. Image it from the top of your head all around you and under your feet. Visualise filling your bubble with gorgeous light and positive energy. In this bubble you are safe and protected – no one can hurt you. It is so peaceful and tranquil.

Visualise what colour this bubble would be, create layers of light or colour and decorate it with anything you wish. Set the intention that you can radiate positive energy out of the bubble but it will not let others negativity through.

Throughout your day, or whenever you feel negativity around check back in, breathe and feel your bubble becoming stronger around you to keep you feeling in control, safe and secure.

Draw your bubble as a reminder – what does it look like...

Repeat after me "TODAY I am willing to let go... I will allow others to focus on whatever is meaningful to them, and I will stay in my own lane and focus on whatever is meaningful to me"

LOVE

love you

Put your hand on your heart.

Feel that?

You are exactly where you are meant to be right now.

Are you being kind to yourself and others?

 **MAKE TIME FOR YOU**

Self care isn't about spa days and holidays, it's how you connect with yourself on a daily basis, how you talk to yourself and care for yourself. It means that you are simply being mindful of your own needs, when you do this, you are better able to support yourself and the people you care about. Self-care comes in a variety of forms.

It can be hard to find time to take care of yourself. However, to be able to live a life you love, it is important to have some "me time."

Ask yourself what activities bring you joy?

These activities do not have to be elaborate or take a lot of planning. It can be something as simple as taking a walk in a park, listening to music, or writing in your journal.

Anything that makes you feel better is worth a little bit of time out of your day.

Hygge is a Danish concept that underlines the importance of focusing on enjoyment in the moment. It's about being present and allowing yourself the time and space to acknowledge a feeling or what's happening now, in the present moment.

It celebrates the little things in life that make life worthwhile such as a cuppa, reading a book, comfy spaces, the feeling of security, home cooked food and time with friends. It lowers stress.

Setting time aside for your self care is key, even 10 minutes sat with a coffee by a lake, or 5 minutes of mindfulness will help you to fill up your cup. You can't give from an empty cup so how will you fill yours?

My cup of self-care

What can I put in my self care cup?
What will I make time to do today?

 **SELF CARE RITUALS**

Two self-care rituals I swear by.

ESSENTIAL OILS
Essential oils are the essence of a plant, distilled and prepared for you to bring the power of nature into your home. Inside many plants hidden in roots, seeds, flowers, bark are concentrated, highly potent chemical compounds. These natural compounds are essential oils. they have the power to support us physically, emotionally, and spiritually.

There are 100's of essential oils and blends. My beautiful friend, Jules Kelly, is my go-to lady for oils. I highly recommend doTERRA oils.

Oils that support self-love are:
Bergamot
Bergamot relieves feelings of despair, self-judgement and low self esteem. It supports individuals in need of self-acceptance and self-love. Bergamot supports you to feel more optimistic.

Rose
Rose oil holds a high vibration. It is a powerful healer of the heart. It supports connection with divine love.

Geranium
Geranium aids in healing the broken heart and supports emotional healing. It restores confidence and encourages love and forgiveness.

Depending which ones you choose, they can be diffused around your home, added to water, included in your diet and applied directly to help your senses and overall well-being.

SALT BATHS
A handful of Himalayan rock salt thrown into your bath helps detoxify. The salt can generate negative ions in the air, creating the type of calming effect many people experience on a salt-water beach. You can even pop a few crystals and essential oil in your bath too.

YOUR MOOD MONITOR

How often are you actually checking in with yourself?

Keeping track of how you feel is super important.

If you are feeling low, what is in your toolkit that can lift your vibe?

A few ways to lift your mood for free...

- Exercising regularly is an important part of staying both physically and mentally healthy. Exercise doesn't have to consist of a complicated workout routine at the gym. It can be as simple as taking the stairs instead of the lift or walking or cycling instead of driving. Daily exercise produces stress-relieving hormones and improves your general health.

- Drinking Water. Two litres a day is the daily recommended amount.

- Eating healthy foods is what will give your body fuel to exercise. By eating mostly unprocessed foods, you can lower your risk for chronic illness and stabilize your energy and mood.

- Getting enough sleep is also important in maintaining your physical and mental health. People generally require seven to nine hours of sleep to stay healthy. Turning off your phone and TV about thirty minutes before you go to bed can help you sleep better.

- Practicing relaxation exercises such as deep breathing and meditation can help reduce stress and clear your mind.

KINDNESS & COMMUNITY

Practising self-care can radiate outwards too, checking in with others and spreading a little love often goes a long way - who can you throw a compliment to today?

"Throw kindness around like confetti"

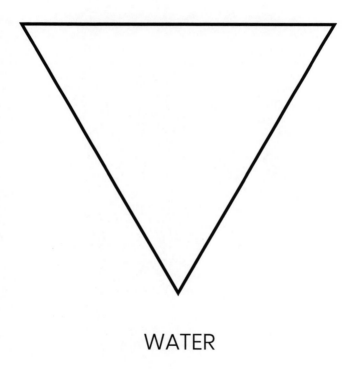

WATER

beautiful
dreamer

Imagine zooming out of all the shoulds and coulds, throwing logic overboard, dreaming yourself as a diver or a mermaid swimming through the ocean.

Time to bring your life plan together and bring your future into your imagination and reality.

 **SELF DISCOVERY**

The world is your oyster and you are the pearl. It's important that you take a look at yourself and truly want out of life. A brilliant way to do this is through Journaling. Grab yourself a beautiful notebook and pen and get started today.

I know it can be hard to know what to write and I want to reassure you that there are no rules. You may prefer to buy a journal that has some structure, or you may be more of a free spirit doodler... There are lots to choose from so go with what is right for you.

A journal will help Learn about yourself and help you organise your thoughts. A journal is an incredible way to help increase confidence and self-awareness can help reduce symptoms of stress and anxiety.

Over the next few pages I have shared some journal prompts to help you.

Uncertainty

Journaling can help you identify and express any difficult and painful emotions even if you have not been consciously aware of them.

It often feels easier to shrug things off to avoid pain and discomfort But these feelings can lie dormant below the surface of your everyday thoughts until you can't keep it back any longer. When it finally comes bubbling up, it may feel more overwhelming than it did originally.

Here are some journal prompts that can help you identify these and bring them to the surface so you can release them

1. Are there any difficult thoughts or emotions that instantly spring to mind right now?

2. What emotions do you find difficult to handle?

3. Are there any regrets you have in life?

4. Are you stressed in life? What is causing it?

5. Are you in a good mood right now? Why?

6. Are you currently hearing any negative self-talk?

7. Who do you speak to about any negative or painful feelings?

8. What are you fearful of?

You don't need to answer all of these, they are designed to help you to uncover some of your more uncomfortable emotions so you can identify what areas can be worked on.

Your Life Loves
Writing about the things that add meaning to your daily life helps you identify what brings you joy.

It can help you focus on gratitude and bring contentment. Understanding what lights, you up can help you focus on bringing more of that into your life.

Here are some prompts to help you.

1. What do you enjoy doing when you are feeling low?

2. What makes you smile?

3. Do you have any daily routines? What are they?

4. How do you relax?

5. Do you show yourself kindness and compassion each day?

6. Do you have any belongings that make you feel happy?

7. Is there a place you go to that makes you feel peaceful?

8. What are your hobbies?

9. Where is your favourite place you have travelled to?

Life Desires
Connecting with who you are also helps unlock a deeper understanding of who you want to become and what you want from life.

Change, growth and transformation is possible.

Time to explore your dreams and desires by creating your potential paths of change:

1. What do you look forward to most in the future?

2. What parts of your life to date has surprised you?

3. What piece of advice would you give to your younger self?

4. What are your goals?

5. Have you any goals that you have already achieved?

6. Are you living the life you want?

7. Do you feel successful?

8. What does successful look like to you?

9. What do you look forward to most in the future?

10. Is there anything you would like to achieve?

11. Do you make time for you?

12. What blocks you from achieving your desires?

Look at your journal - is there anything negative? How can you flip that to the opposite and create a positive?
Look at the positives, these can start to form your Life Plan Vision.

* _____

* _____

* _____

* _____

* _____

* _____

* _____

* _____

* _____

* _____

* _____

 **VISUALISATION**

There are lots of ways you can use visualisation, you can journal your dreams, you can draw them out, there are lots of meditations that can help you visualise what you desire.

Getting yourself into a quiet place switches off from all the noise and internal mind chatter and lets your imagination flow. Whether it is words, doodles or simply a vision.

- How do you see your life?

- If anything is possible, what would it look like?

- If you were to take a magic wand and transform your life - how would it be?

- Think about what you can start with today to take step closer towards this life. How can you dress?

- Where will you shop?

- What will you eat?

- How can organise your home?

- Where will you go?

- What will you do?

Start today

Think about the new version of you and things can change straight away.

If the new you always buys flowers. Get out and grab yourself a bunch today.

The new you has gorgeous underwear. Time to fling out the old knickers and embrace the new.

You want a new beautiful bedroom with fitted wardrobes.

Today declutter your room, give away to charity or sell clothes that no longer serve you.

Your future self will give to charity. Starting today, can you volunteer? What can you clear out and donate that you already have?

You will live in a beautiful home. How can you tidy and clean where you are, can you move furniture around to change the energy and the 'feel' of the place

You want to go on a spa day but can't book one yet?

Take action today, create your own spa and sanctuary at home, or go for a swim or walk, anything you can start to do to step into your new way of 'being'.

 **DESIGN YOUR DREAM**

Get two pieces of paper one green one red.

I like to cut mine in a star shape. On the red star write everything you do not like in your life right now, from clients, relationships, job, money worries, concerns, angst – as much as you can think of.

Take the green star – write on this everything you love and would like to attract into your life.

Time to call in the new and let the rest go...

Once you are done take the green star and pin it somewhere you can see it – on a mirror or door or your desk.

Take the red star and screw it up in a ball and throw it away or take it out in the garden and burn it.

YOUR VISION BOARD

A vision board, is where you can truly start to bring your vision to life in the form of a collage that you can connect with daily.

To get started decide what size you would like it. Mine is on a huge A3 canvas but you may want something smaller that you can keep personal inside a notebook – the choice is yours.

On your board you can identify all the things you would like to bring to life. For example, it maybe material things like:

The car you would like, the home you would like to live in, the holiday you would like to go on, places you would like to visit.

It may have a FEELINGS SECTION with pictures that make you feel, happy, loved, healthy

It can contain images of your family, friends.

And affirmation and intentions for what you would like to achieve.

There are really no rules but there are plenty of choices in how you can present them on your board.

You can have sections for LOVE, HEALTH, FAMILY. HOME or may want to just create a collage of photos or words.

I use a fabulous model created by the lovely Sarah Stone. In her book she explains feng shui and how you can create a vision board and then bring it to life around your home.

Whatever style you use, take a look at it every day, connect to how it makes you feel. When you achieve one of your desires, be sure to take it down and thank yourself and the universe. Practicing gratitude is key to manifesting your future goals and desires. Ensure you add new things as your life grows and expands too.

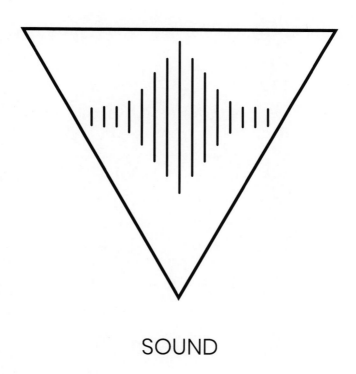

SOUND

good vibes

Communication, creativity listening, being heard sharing ideas. High vibe attracts positive flow, when we can lift our vibe, it lifts our energy and the universe will respond. Living a high vibe, happy life oozes positivity.

 **HONESTY**

Know when you need to ask for help. In life, it's easy to become overwhelmed. Being overwhelmed does not make you any less of a person. It doesn't make you weak. It makes you human.   It makes you STRONG. The ability to speak up and be able to own your emotions – all of them is one of the strongest most powerful things you can do.

MUSIC & MOVEMENT

Create a playlist of your favourite high vibe tunes, blast them out at every opportunity and celebrate life. Dance along with life, soak it all up, sing it out louder than ever before... Attract it in.

"What's on your playlist?"

AMPLIFYING YOUR THOUGHTS

They say a problem shared is a problem halved, equally sharing new ideas, thoughts and visions with friends, colleagues and mentors is an incredible way to increase your positivity, surrounding yourself with like minded souls can help increase your vibe.

Not Everybody deserves to be part of your circle of friends.

Be choosy about who you let into your life if you want to keep thriving and enjoying your life.

Who you surround yourself with is either elevating you and taking you higher, or they are depleting your energy and bringing you down. High vibe attracts high vibe so surround yourself with those people who make you feel good and are going to lift you higher.

 **YOUR VOICE**

What are you communicating to yourself?

The words you say to yourself are powerful. Often you can be very unkind to yourself and the things you tell yourself. Imagine saying some of those things to someone you love?

It's time to start to reframe using loving and compassionate words to yourself.

Use the speech bubble – what are you telling yourself today? Is it negative? How can you turn this positive?

Notes to self will become your daily reminder to you.

Grab a post it note and pen and create yourself some affirmations.

Here's some ideas to choose from...

I am enough

I am safe

I am grateful today

I release all that doesn't serve me

I believe in me

I am at peace with me today

I cherish myself

I am worthy

Today I focus on the present moment

I can forgive people easily.

It's ok to relax and let it go

Today I believe in me

I remain strong when things go wrong

I am beautiful

Post them around your home, inside your diary, on your mirror, in the fridge, wherever they will catch your eye throughout the day..

SPACE

Spirituality is the recognition that there is something greater than yourself, something more to being human and than sensory experience, it's a belief that the greater whole of which we are part is cosmic or divine in nature.

This element helps us with understanding and wisdom.

 ## ENERGY HEALING

Energy healing is a holistic practice that activates the body's subtle energy systems to remove blocks. By breaking through these energetic blocks, the body's inherent ability to heal itself is stimulated.

Chakras
If you've ever taken a yoga or meditation class, had an energy healing session like reiki, you've no doubt heard about chakras and the role they play in the flow of energy in your body.

You may have also learned that it's important to keep your chakras open or unblocked and there are several ways you can do this. "chakra" means "disk" or "wheel" and refers to the energy centres in your body. These wheels or disks of spinning energy each correspond to certain nerve bundles and major organs.

To function at their best, your chakras need to stay open, or balanced. If they get blocked, you may experience physical or emotional symptoms related to a particular chakra.

There are seven main chakras that run along your spine. They start at the root, or base, of your spine and extend to the crown of your head.

Root chakra
The root chakra is located at the base of your spine. It provides you with a base or foundation for life, and it helps you feel grounded and able to withstand challenges. Your root chakra is responsible for your sense of security and stability.

Sacral chakra
The sacral chakra is located just below your belly button. This chakra is responsible for your sexual and creative energy. It's also linked to how you relate to your emotions as well as the emotions of others.

Solar plexus chakra
The solar plexus chakra is located in your stomach area. It's responsible for confidence and self-esteem, as well as helping you feel in control of your life.

Heart chakra
The heart chakra is located near your heart, in the centre of your chest. The heart chakra is all about our ability to love and show compassion.

Throat chakra
The throat chakra is located in your throat. This chakra connects with our ability to communicate verbally.

Third eye chakra
The third eye chakra is located between your eyes which is responsible for intuition and imagination.

Crown chakra
The crown chakra is located at the top of your head and represents your spiritual connection to yourself, others, and the universe. It also plays a role in your life's purpose.

There are five warning signs that your chakras might be out of balance. The goal is to feel harmonious and to do that we need balance. Ask yourself right now.

1. Does something feel 'off'

2. Do I feel Sick

3. Have I had repeated illness?

4. Am I struggling to concentrate and making mistakes?

5. Does everything seem to be falling apart?

Where did you feel the response in your body? Your chakra may well need a little balancing and there are many ways that you can do this. The use of crystals is powerful as is meditation, breath work and essential oils.

Reiki is an energy healing technique that promotes relaxation, reduces stress and anxiety through gentle touch. Reiki practitioners use their hands to deliver energy to your body, improving the flow and balance of your energy to support healing.

Reiki can help clear and rebalance your chakras

EFT

Emotional freedom technique (EFT) is an alternative treatment for physical pain and emotional distress. It's also referred to as tapping or psychological acupressure.

You can use this technique to create a balance in your energy system and treat pain. It's an easy-to-learn technique that involves "tapping" on the meridian points or energy hot spots — to restore balance to your body's energy.

When we restore this energy balance, it can also relieve symptoms from a negative experience or emotion may have while repeating statements that help us focus on an issue from which we want to seek relief from.

 **MOON & STARS**

Moon Magic
Is a special type of astrology that uses the moon to create the life you long for?

By working with the phases of the moon you can learn to apply her magic in your life. The Moon represents powerful feminine energy. It signifies wisdom, intuition, birth, death, reincarnation, and a spiritual connection. Moon cycles are similar to the cycle of a seed: the seed grows into a flower, then blooms, and then dies or lays dormant to start to repeat the cycle again

The moon is powerful, it controls the tides of the ocean, and we are made up of sixty per cent water, we can feel it's movement in everyday life.

New Moon - PLANT YOUR SEEDS
During a new moon cycle, you can work on calling in the new. Making wishes for yourself and others. This is a really good time for you to write down your wishes and intentions

The Waxing Crescent Moon - EXPLORE
This is the time to keep the faith and to have courage. If you want something, you have to chase it.

The First Quarter Moon: - COMMIT
This is a really important time to go back and re-read the wish lists you made at the time of the New Moon. Re-feel them. Re-visualize them. Re-imagine them.

Gibbous Moon - STAY ON COURSE
Stay open to whatever life is teaching you. If you know you need to make some changes to achieve your goals, make them now.

Full Moon - LETTING GO
Full moon is the best time that you can work on releasing negativity and forgiveness and focus on what you are thankful for, practicing gratitude.

The Disseminating Moon - BREATHE
The more you can accept 'what is', the better your emotional health.

The Third Quarter Moon - ENQUIRE
This is also a very good time to break bad habits. You're at a turning point so the question is, 'Which way do you want to turn?' Are you sticking with your old plans or making new ones?

The Balsamic Moon - RELEASE
Time for rest and healing. Give yourself a break. Daydream. Dream big. Go wild in your imagination. Smile to yourself.

Astrology

Astrology is the study of the movement and positioning of the stars and planets around the earth. A zodiac sign is a symbol that represents somebody's personality, emotions, and motivations. Everybody has many different signs, one for each planet, the moon, the sun, and many more.

There are lots of ways you can use astrology in daily life, from a simple star sign to looking at the positing of the stars and planets at the time of your birth and a full human design reading.

I happen to be a typical Aquarian

Quirky and free-thinking but can be super stubborn. A rule breaker and I don't like to be told what to do and struggle to admit I'm wrong.

What Star Sign are you?

Is this reflective of you?

Want to learn more? – The Inner Sky by Stephen Forrest takes an in depth look at how astrology impacts the individual person that you are.

 **YOUR HIGHER SELF**

Your Higher Self is the real you, the soul consciousness that is much more than your physical body. Your Higher Self is the 'you' that is unlimited. It's the part of you that excites you with inspiration and guides you with intuition, it teaches you through insight. Your higher self knows your intentions, desires, and your secrets

I know you probably know everything about yourself, but have you ever had a conversation with your higher self?

Have you ever had useful flashes of intuition or inspiration?

Well they can become a much bigger part of your life if you explore more and allow this communication to grow.

When you can rise above your own life and look at it from a place of service to others, you ignite your divine essence from within and become the higher version of yourself.

With conscious attention, you can learn to access your higher consciousness, or the spiritual self, with greater frequency.

Now I know this might all sound a bit 'off the wall' many call it 'woo' however, I have become increasing spiritual over the last 10 years and love spending time reading tarot and oracle cards, quieting my mind through meditation and listening in to their guidance and it had been a huge part of my transformation.

I make no secret of the fact that I connect with spirit guides and angels on a daily basis. I have also used AWE writing during the writing of this book, when words have literally been channelled through me onto the pages. Now I know you may be sceptical and that's ok, I'm a big believer that everyone has their own opinion and choice on this but it has been absolutely life changing for me so I am beyond proud to share it with you in my tool box.

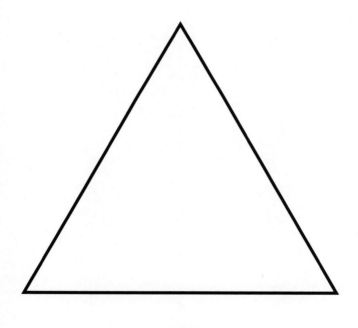

FIRE

intention &
activation...

How can you rise? Personal power, assertiveness, transformation.

How can you activate a new life?

Igniting your passion for the future.

For success with manifestation, you have to meet the energetic vibration, set intentions and believe that it will become reality, then take active steps towards making that idea come to fruition into reality

 **CLEARING SPACE**

If you are feeling negative or your home feels like it needs clearing incense is a great way to do this. Sage is a brilliant space clearer.

Before you start, take some time to contemplate what your wishes are for your home and family. When you clear your house, there's a vacuum that's created. You want to welcome your intentions into the newly cleared and open space.

Smudging the Space
Now that you have all your tools and preparations in place, you can begin the smudging ritual.

Start at the front door of your home and light your incense or smudge stick. Then, begin to move around your home. Move mindfully and with care, walking clockwise around the entire perimeter of the home. Be sure to allow the smoke to drift into the hidden spaces.

When you arrive back at your front door. Visualise the entire home is filled with bright white sunlight.

SUNSHINE OF GRATITUDE

Creating your own gratitude daily helps you focus on a magnetic energy when manifesting your life's desires. Being grateful can flip your mood from negativity into positivity and deep appreciation

Make it a Ritual
Think about how you can make time to do this, so it becomes a habit – a time that you look forward to. Some people like to do it morning or evening but be consistent with your practice.

Treat yourself to a beautiful notebook and pen and when you are writing you could grab a cuppa in your favourite mug or pop on a beautiful song that make you feel happy. Sit somewhere comfortably and make it as cosy experience as possible.

Start writing... You can stick to a fixed number, i.e. Today I am grateful for these 5 things.

Or you can let your writing flow for everything that you are super grateful for.

Even when you are having a rubbish day, you can always thank your future self for achieving your potential desires too.

Not sure where to get started? Here are some examples of gratitude:

- Thank you for my beautiful home.
- I am so blessed to have a warm bed, a cuppa and to feel safe and warm today.
- Thank you for my daughters for us all being healthy and happy today.
- I really appreciate my creativity and knowledge
- Thank you for the money.

You can also use senses and thoughts too.

What do you love, what do you see, what can you smell, what can you hear?

 **IGNITING INTENTION WITH AFFIRMATIONS**

Affirmations are an amazing way to start believing in yourself and what is possible, what you tell yourself on a daily basis is key. Your affirmations can be as short as one word to a full statement about how you want to feel or what you would like to achieve.

It's important when setting your affirmations that you anchor into the belief that you already have it here and now.

Affirmations can help you transform your life, used on a regular basis they allow you to start embracing self-acceptance and learning to love yourself, they help you anchor into achieving a life of your dreams and desires and are key to manifesting a life you love.

You can use affirmation cards or you can write your own intentional affirmations. Here are some ideas for you:

LOVE
- I attract my perfect partner
- I deserve a loving partner
- I am in a loving relationship
- My relationship are harmonious and balanced

LIFE
- I live a life that I love
- I am happy in my life
- My life if filled with joy and happiness
- I am living my best life and make the most of everyday

HEALTH
- I am healthy
- I feel good in my body
- I am beautiful
- I feel good about myself today

MONEY

- I have more than enough money
- Money comes to me easily
- I have everything I need
- I am wealthy
- I manifest money with ease and grace

BUSINESS

- My business is hugely successful
- I have balance in my business that allows me to enjoy all aspects of my life
- I attract new clients easily
- My business is blooming

POSITIVITY

- I feel happy and free
- My life feels full of joy
- All I need is within me right now
- I can achieve anything I want to

MINDSET

- I am enough
- I believe in me
- I am worthy
- I am strong
- Ways to anchor in your affirmations
- Write them on your hand
- Write them on post it notes
- Put notes in a jar and draw one out each day
- Write them on cards
- Wear affirmation jewellery
- Wear it on your clothing (i have a range of affirmation clothing)
- Record it on your phone
- Have it as a screen savers
- Hang a picture of it around your home
- Journal it
- Sing it out loud
- Add it to you vision board
- If it's one you want to keep permanently you can even wear it as a tattoo

light it up...

LIGHTING UP YOUR LIFE

One way which I love to activate intention is by literally lighting it up. So repeating the affirmation or intention, striking a match and lighting a candle.

When you do this, you can focus on the flame, visualise your future self, think about where you are now and anchor in the possibility of you achieving your desires. See the light as your hope and possibility for your future. Leave it burning as long as you wish and when you blow it out close your eyes and imagine it is already within you.

Then allow a sense of gratitude to flow through you.

THE HAND OF POSSIBILITY

Take your hand.

Draw around your hand. Write on each finger.

1. I never thought I would... but I did

2. Next finger, younger me, would never................, but I have.

3. Middle finger, breath. Imagine what is possible in your life. Set an intention

4. Next finger. Write I could never................, but the future me will ....,

5. Think of the future

We carry our hand wherever we go so if you are ever feeling not good enough, feeling judged, feeling like you can't do it, I want to you hold your hand and take it in those 5 steps .

From impossible to I'm possible

Without limit.

All of it.

You are limitless.

SPACE TO DRAW YOUR OWN HAND OF POSSIBILITY

PART 3

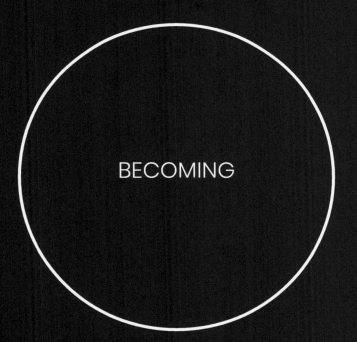

BECOMING

"Rise Up" by Andra Day

Over the last eleven years I have rebuilt so much of my life, I have used my life tools and I have done the work. I have found the courage to live on my own with my girls, I have learned to love myself. I have navigated a tsunami of life's curveballs and to got comfortable with uncertainty.

I was looking for some notes to share with you from my journals about 'becoming 'who I am' I have many journals and one jumped out at me off the shelf. I picked it up and it as if by magic fell open at the page from exactly a year ago.

This time last year, we were in the middle of lockdown during the pandemic and my dad had been really ill and they had started end of life care. I had written in my journal about my feelings of emptiness and overwhelm. And I had allowed myself to step back from work and my daily duties, to soak up the sunshine outside.

I had spent time on my self care and development, and I was aware I needed healing. I had also journaled about my ideas and 'why' for my new product range (I just love the synergy of the universe, the fact I am bringing it to life exactly one year on.) And I had taken myself back into notes of my earlier married life days with the realisation that I had become so much more...

That I had discovered myself, that I understood myself and felt a sense of inner happy even through this traumatic of times.

The realisation that I have my own uniqueness and I am here to be seen, here to shine my light so I can help and support others to find theirs and to enable them to see during their own darkness.

My dad was diagnosed with a terminal illness shortly after I lost my brother. It robbed him of his independence.

I grieved for my dad whilst he was still alive, I thought I had prepared for the loss of him in my physical world.

When he finally passed away, I thought I would be ok.

I was wrong.

The day he passed – it hit me like a steam train, and I was really not ok.

Why?

Because not only did I lose him, but it also triggered my grief cycle from my past loss and trauma and my dad leaving the physical world made me feel really alone.

The stark reality that I had lost both my parents made my inner child scream in pain. A friend described it as becoming an adult orphan

Alone and abandoned

And my beautiful girls, with no grandparents.

So, what did I do?

I acknowledged that I was not ok. I took time out; I used my life tools, and I once again did the inner work.
My Dad loved to garden so I anchored into what I could, and I stepped outside.
I grounded, I felt into my sadness, I spent many mindful moments looking at plants and nature, I planted seeds to anchor into possibility as I knew that would bloom in my future.

I made my garden a sanctuary and I spent time with my closest friends and my beautiful family. My sisters and my daughters have been a tower of strength and support for me, and I became truly thankful for all I have in my life.

Orange butterflies would follow me - I would smile, a little reminder from my dad that I held everything within to truly create a life I love

And like a caterpillar I cocooned.

I wrapped myself in self care.

Until I was ready to awaken and step out with a decision that I was going to make the very best of the rest of my life. A life that would feel fulfilled, one filled with joy, happiness, travel and new experiences.

The time was 'now'. This was my project life reset.

I made the decision that I was going to go all in and "Drink Life While It's Fizzy"®.

I allowed the transformative energies of fate to expand my life experience.

I made a choice to learn, to practice patience and determination, to become the person I wanted to be, the very best version of me. And to create change for the greater good.

I stepped outside of conformity and well-meaning advice. I gave myself permission to get creative, to get curious, to have fun, and to play.

New shifts started to emerge, new ideas popped in my head and the energy felt amazing and aligned.

I started to believe in myself more than ever before.
To trust that my success is possible.
To know that I am enough and worthy.
To understand that energy is key and that I have very special guides. that walk through this life with me.

"Non action allows for dreams to come true"

Space gave me time and reflection. The possibilities of life are limitless.

I could hear the message loud and clear " to turn poor me into positivity".

To provide tools and support so I could help others heal themselves whilst giving back to charities that helped support others too.

To create small steps to create change, to support healing vibes and positive energy.

Through the lighting of a candle, to holding a crystal, to wearing clothing that feels like a hug. All to help and support others' own journey of self-discovery.

I wanted to support YOU.
To create your own inner knowing that… You are enough
That you have always been enough and that you always will be enough
That you are worthy of whatever you desire.

It's time to dream big, to shine bright.
You are the creator of your own reality.

What story are you telling yourself right now?

It's time to live a life without fearing the outcome. A life filled with freedom, hope, peace, love, courage and possibility.

Ask yourself… if I knew everything would be ok, what would I do?

"Firework" by Katy Perry

PEACE, CALM & TRANQUILLITY

I want you to live a life in full bloom, one where you create a true sense of inner peace.

What makes you feel an inner sense of calm?
.
.
.
Do more of that.

Side note: Exploring my creativity, being curious in the everyday, dreaming big, having fun with my thoughts and imagination. My guiding light, my inner voice, connection with my knowing and wisdom, knowledge and strength has given me this.

FREEDOM & FAITH

Imagine a life where the water is calmer
Where you choose your own free will, now and through your lifetime and through all your layers of being (releasing shame, fear, judgment, guilt, ridicule and suffering)
A life of being yourself.. individual, being you, being different, expressing who you truly are

Repeat after me.. I choose to forgive and free myself unconditionally today.

I give myself full permission to have...

- Freedom of choice

- Freedom to feel

- Freedom to expand

- Freedom to speak

The freedom to explore the world like a child.

Think about the elemental energies and how they can inspire you.

CONNECTION
Look at the relationships you surround yourself with.
Connect with others that share the same values as you

TRUST, LOVE, RESPECT
Choose who you want to be and who you want to join you to dance through this beautiful life with.

RECONNECT - RECOMMIT AND RECLAIM YOUR POWER
Call it all back to you, accept yourself for who you are and learn to receive - you deserve all that you dream of.

YOUR LIGHT OF POSSIBILITY

Fully embrace your own creativity and light. Fill your life with things that light you up and fill you with joy.

Becoming a living inspiration is a lifestyle choice.

Surround yourself with things that are beautiful and feed your soul and that make you smile.

> "I will surround myself with beautiful things – that will be my life."

Step into the limelight of your own possibility and potential, allow yourself to feel this energy so that you can grow and expand

What lights you up?

It's time to fully step into your own spotlight of possibility.

Spend time in the sunlight, feel it on your face.

THE STAR THAT YOU ARE

Becoming the true, authentic you, listen to your heart, how does it feel?
Fall in love with your own story. Accept full responsibility as the author of your own life.

Step outside, look at the stars – see that? The universe is a vast space of infinite possibility filled with hope.

It is limitless and so are you.

Look up, connect to your star and start to live your life to the full as you truly are. You are ready to rise.

BELIEVE IN YOUR RAINBOWS

Be one step ahead.

Strive for one per cent better each day. Form the habits to create the change and take one step at a time.

Let go of the need to get to a 'final destination' today, life doesn't work that way.

Just BREATHE and remember you are amazing, you are doing great and YOU'VE GOT THIS.

Where you are right now is the perfectly timed place, you are exactly where you should be, you are safe and you are loved right in this moment.

You only have the here and NOW. The present moment is where you are and the next step is what will help you create change.

Notice the wonderful life you have already and think about what you have overcome to get here. You have all the time you need and anything is possible.

LOVE

Draw the Line under the past.

A shift from trauma, turmoil, grief, hurt, pain, angst, to one of healing, help, support, strength, hope, dreaming and possibility.

I got there with gratitude for where I was on my path of life.

Doing the inner work, going within and getting support, a journey of healing and hope. Building my strength and resilience so that I could shift, so that I could transform so that I could believe in possibility and positivity and live in the flow of life and focus on my dreams. The realisation that I am my own, very special, unique self. The one and only me. Perfectly imperfect in every way.

So, what are you fearing right now?
How are you not stepping into your own light?
Is it the fear of judgment, fear of not being heard, not wanted, rejected?

Think about the fear.

Then set your intention to shine through.
To become proud of who you are.
To refuse to make yourself small.
To be your own lighthouse.

It's time for you to wish upon your own star. Setting your intentions based on your dreams, desires and aspirations.

Your dreams can totally become your reality.

Love is what will set you free.

What do you desire?

It's time to find your own peace, harmony and happiness.

"Let It Be" by The Beatles

THE COURAGE TO OPEN UP AND ALLOW THE TRANSFORMATION

Shine the brightest of light upon yourself so you can see you in your full glory.

Letting go of your past and your old stories.

Opening up and trusting in yourself.

Pushing beyond your perceived limitations.

YOUR INNER CHILD
The voice of your inner child can often be where we hold ourselves back, but it also the place that we can connect, learn to lighten up, to simplify things and to live in joy.

When you were a child, what did you like to do?

For me it was simple things like counting money, playing a board game, rearranging my bedroom, colouring in and playing with dolls.

I was comfortable with who I was back then, before all the layers of conditioning. What did you used to do? is there anything you can do today to bring your inner child out to play?

The only people with any power to judge, control or hold you back from your destiny are those that you empower to do so. At any moment you can free yourself from their influence over you, by making a choice to love yourself unconditionally.

Your path and your purpose are as unique and individual as you are.

It's time to stay in your own lane and water your own garden.

YOUR NEW HORIZON

WHAT'S ON YOUR HORIZON?
A life filled with...
Fulfilment
Security and peace
Togetherness
Love and compassion
Satisfaction
Success and drive
Possibility and motivation
Hope and dreams

IT'S TIME TO PLAN YOUR ROUTE
Your seed of life is bursting open to show you the way.
What seeds have you planted that will start to breakthrough?
What do you need to let go to open the gates of your epic life?
What needs to happen for you to create a life you truly love?

PRACTICE GRATITUDE BY SAYING
I live a balanced and blessed life.
I treasure each day and I am grateful for who I share it with.
I am love.
I am me.
I am.

DESIGN A LIFE YOU LOVE

Commit to your vision. Trust that your dreams can become reality
Wish upon a star.
Celebrate you.
Believe you can achieve absolutely anything you want to and create a new reality.
It starts today and everyday you can take action to be one step closer to your desires.

TAKE INSPIRED ACTION

Be different.
Think different.
You are different.
You are uniquely you.
It starts with you.
Ride your waves of possibility.
Be the creator of your dream life.
Stay anchored in the flow.
Keep being curious every day.

LIVE IN YOUR OWN LIGHT

When you connect to your own inner light something truly magical happens. Your strength becomes anchored, your hopes and dreams start to feel like possibilities and your inspired action will start to flow.
Step inside yourself, it's a beautiful place to be, when you can open up your heart and create your own happiness within.

A NEW AGE

Tend to your seeds.
Keeping your focus fixed.
The world needs more people with hope in their heart.
We need to radiate this energy on a global level.
The seas ahead may not be plain sailing, a new age never is.
It's time to keep holding your vision.
You have everything you need in your heart and your heart is your home.

HOPE FOR YOU & OTHERS

"May we love within all layers of our being and radiate that love so that every being can be happy and free."

Naomi Victoria

I have nurtured the seeds, I have watched them grow and my garden of legacy is this... my book and my product ranges.

Writing my book and developing my new product ranges has activated my healing and allowed me to create a movement of change, to stop the stigmas around mental health, to support the charities in their valuable work, and to signpost those who need it to get support to change their lives.

CHANGE TAKES COURAGE
We must be willing to let go of what we have known and experience uncertainty whilst we hold on to hope and explore possibility and then and only then can we emerge into a new way of being.

IT'S TIME TO LET GO OF THE PAST, TO EMBRACE YOUR LIFE'S LEGACY

TO LOVE YOURSELF AND LIVE A LIFE YOU LOVE

THE END...
OH NO IT'S NOT!
THIS IS YOUR NEW

beginning

♪

"New Dawn" by Michael Bublé

With Gratitude

To my beautiful girls, Molly and Ruby, for always being by my side and forever in my heart. Thank you for all the love and light you shine on my world. I love you to the moon and back (and all around the world).

To my gorgeous sisters, Sarah and Rachel, thank you for holding my hand and being my rock along the journey we have often navigated together, and to my big brother, Alistair, for being there to lean on when I need you. You have all been here since the beginning, experiencing some of our darkest times together. Without you all, there would have been times when holding on to hope would have been so much harder.

To my fabulous friend Vicki, not only did you encourage me to write this book. You have held my hand every step of the way, always believed in me and inspire me every single day. Thank you for working your unique magic and bringing this book to life.

To my dear friend Debbie, thank you for opening my own world of possibility and positivity and for walking this path with me.

To my joyous friend Jules, for not only being an all-round gorgeous human, for making me belly laugh (lots) and for all your hands on help and support too!

Thank you to my online community, friends and family, to all of you, for believing in me and my vision to bring change to the world, I am truly grateful to have you in mine.

Naomi Victoria x

BOOK REFERENCES

Brené Brown: www.brenebrown.com
Kubler Ross: www.ekrfoundation.org
Wim Hoff: www.wimhofmethod.com
Yasmin Boland: www.yasminboland.com
Rebecca Campbell: www.rebeccacampbell.me
Sarah Stone: www.sarahstone.com

SUPPORT & RESOURCES

Scan the QR code to access more resources.

PERSONALLY POSITIVE

Throughout the book I referred to using physical products to uplift and inspire you in everyday life. Personally Positive proudly supports mental health and suicide prevention charities.

www.personallypositive.com

ABOUT THE AUTHOR

Naomi Victoria is a Motivational speaker, mental health awareness and suicide prevention advocate and the founder of Personally Positive. She inspires others to understand that no matter what happens in life you can create your inner happy.

A successful entrepreneur and business owner, Naomi believes in loving yourself and loving life and shares this through her lessons of hope and possibility.

Naomi guides others to believe in themselves and become who they were born to be.

Printed in Great Britain
by Amazon